بسم الله الرحمن الرحيم

ABOUT THE AUTHOR

The author, who writes under the pen-name HARUN YAHYA, was born in Ankara in 1956. Having completed his primary and secondary education in Ankara, he then studied arts at Istanbul's Mimar Sinan University and philosophy at Istanbul University. Since the 1980s, the author has published many books on political, faith-related and scientific issues. Harun Yahya is well-known as an author who has written very important works disclosing the imposture of evolutionists, the invalidity of their claims and the dark liaisons between Darwinism and bloody ideologies such as fascism and communism.

His pen-name is made up of the names "Harun" (Aaron) and "Yahya" (John), in memory of the two esteemed prophets who fought against lack of faith. The Prophet's seal, may Allah bless him and grant him peace, on the cover of the books is symbolic and is linked to the their contents. It represents the Qur'an (the final scripture) and the Prophet Muhammad, may Allah bless him and grant him peace, the last of the prophets. Under the guidance of the Qur'an and sunnah, the author makes it his purpose to disprove each one of the fundamental tenets of godless ideologies and to have the "last word", so as to completely silence the objections raised against religion. The seal of the final Prophet, who attained ultimate wisdom and moral perfection, is used as a sign of his intention of saying this last word.

All author's works center around one goal: to convey the Qur'an's message to people, encourage them to think about basic faith-related issues (such as the existence of Allah, His unity and the hereafter), and to expose the feeble foundations and perverted ideologies of godless systems.

Harun Yahya enjoys a wide readership in many countries, from India to America, England to Indonesia, Poland to Bosnia, and Spain to Brazil. Some of his books are available in English, French, German, Spanish, Italian, Portuguese, Urdu, Arabic, Albanian, Russian, Serbo-Croat (Bosnian), Polish, Malay, Uygur Turkish, and Indonesian, and they are enjoyed by readers worldwide.

Greatly appreciated all around the world, these works have been instrumental in many people recovering their faith in Allah and in many others gaining a deeper insight into their faith. The wisdom, and the sincere and easy-to-understand style gives these books a distinct touch which directly effects any one who reads or studies them. Immune to objections, these works are characterized by their features of rapid effectiveness, definite results and irrefutability. It is unlikely that those who read these books and give serious thought to them can any longer sincerely advocate the materialistic philosophy, atheism or any other perverted ideology or philosophy. Even if they continue to do so, it will be only a sentimental insistence since these books refuted such ideologies from their very foundations. All contemporary movements of denial are now ideologically defeated, thanks to the collection of books written by Harun Yahya.

There is no doubt that these features result from the wisdom and lucidity of the Qur'an. The author modestly intends to serve as a means in humanity's search for Allah's right path. No material gain is sought in the publication of these works.

Considering these facts, those who encourage people to read these books, which open the "eyes" of the heart and guide them to become more devoted servants of Allah, render an invaluable service.

Meanwhile, it would just be a waste of time and energy to propagate other books which create confusion in peoples' minds, lead man into ideological chaos, and which, clearly have no strong and precise effects in removing the doubts in peoples' hearts, as also verified from previous experience. It is apparent that it is impossible for books devised to emphasize the author's literary power rather than the noble goal of saving people from loss of faith, to have such a great effect. Those who doubt this can readily see that the sole aim of Harun Yahya's books is to overcome disbelief and to disseminate the moral values of the Qur'an. The success and impact of this service are manifest in readers' conviction.

One point should be kept in mind: The main reason for the continuing cruelty, conflict, and all the ordeals the majority of people undergo is the ideological prevalence of disbelief. This state can only be ended with the ideological defeat of disbelief and by conveying the wonders of creation and Qur'anic morality so that people can live by it. Considering the state of the world today, which leads people into the downward spiral of violence, corruption and conflict, it is clear that this service has to be provided more speedily and effectively. Otherwise, it may be too late.

It is no exaggeration to say that the collection of books by Harun Yahya have assumed this leading role. By the will of Allah, these books will be a means through which people in the 21st century will attain the peace, justice and happiness promised in the Qur'an.

CHILDREN!
HAVE YOU EVER THOUGHT?
-3-

wonderful
creatures

HARUN YAHYA

March, 2003

www.harunyahya.com / www.for-children.com / www.truthforkids.com
info@harunyahya.com / info@for-children.com / info@truthforkids.com

TO THE READER

● In all the books by the author, faith-related issues are explained in the light of Qur'anic verses, and people are invited to learn Allah's words and to live by them. All the subjects that concern Allah's verses are explained in such a way as to leave no room for doubt or question marks in the reader's mind. The sincere, plain and fluent style employed ensures that everyone of every age and from every social group can easily understand the books. This effective and lucid narrative makes it possible to read them in a single sitting. Even those who rigorously reject spirituality are influenced by the facts recounted in these books and cannot refute the truthfulness of their contents.

● This book and all the other works by Harun Yahya can be read individually or discussed in a group. Those readers who are willing to profit from the books will find discussion very useful in that they will be able to relate their own reflections and experiences to one another.

● In addition, it is a great service to the religion to contribute to the presentation and circulation of these books, which are written solely for the good pleasure of Allah. All the books of the author are extremely convincing, so, for those who want to communicate the religion to other people, one of the most effective methods is to encourage them to read these books.

● It is hoped that the reader will take time to look through the review of other books on the final pages of the book, and appreciate the rich source of material on faith-related issues, which are very useful and a pleasure to read.

● In them, one will not find, as in some other books, the personal views of the author, explanations based on dubious sources, styles unobservant of the respect and reverence due to sacred subjects, or hopeless, doubt-creating, and pessimistic accounts that create deviations in the heart.

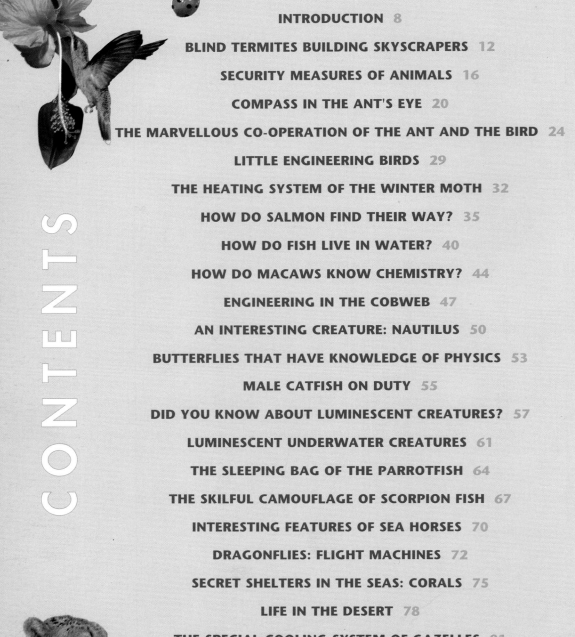

CONTENTS

INTRODUCTION 8

BLIND TERMITES BUILDING SKYSCRAPERS 12

SECURITY MEASURES OF ANIMALS 16

COMPASS IN THE ANT'S EYE 20

THE MARVELLOUS CO-OPERATION OF THE ANT AND THE BIRD 24

LITTLE ENGINEERING BIRDS 29

THE HEATING SYSTEM OF THE WINTER MOTH 32

HOW DO SALMON FIND THEIR WAY? 35

HOW DO FISH LIVE IN WATER? 40

HOW DO MACAWS KNOW CHEMISTRY? 44

ENGINEERING IN THE COBWEB 47

AN INTERESTING CREATURE: NAUTILUS 50

BUTTERFLIES THAT HAVE KNOWLEDGE OF PHYSICS 53

MALE CATFISH ON DUTY 55

DID YOU KNOW ABOUT LUMINESCENT CREATURES? 57

LUMINESCENT UNDERWATER CREATURES 61

THE SLEEPING BAG OF THE PARROTFISH 64

THE SKILFUL CAMOUFLAGE OF SCORPION FISH 67

INTERESTING FEATURES OF SEA HORSES 70

DRAGONFLIES: FLIGHT MACHINES 72

SECRET SHELTERS IN THE SEAS: CORALS 75

LIFE IN THE DESERT 78

THE SPECIAL COOLING SYSTEM OF GAZELLES 81

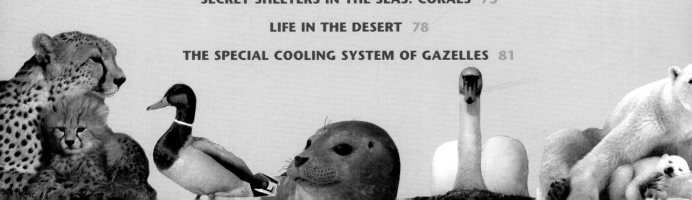

CONTENTS

THE STRENGTH OF WOODPECKERS 83

CUTE SQUIRRELS WITH BIG CHEEKS 86

THE BIRD WITH THE LONGEST WINGS OF THE WORLD: THE ALBATROSS 87

ADORNMENT ARTISTS: BOWERBIRDS 90

BIRDS WHICH LAY FOUNDATIONS FOR THEIR YOUNG 92

THE POWERFUL MEMORY OF JAYS 95

THE ARMOURED TANKS OF THE ANIMAL KINGDOM 96

MIGRATORY BIRDS THAT CAN FLY EVEN IN THE DARK OF THE NIGHT 97

CLEANING WORKERS OF THE SEAS 100

THE NOISY CICADA 102

CLEANER BIRDS 103

POND SKATERS THAT WALK ON WATER 104

TENACIOUS SUCKERFISH 105

WALKING FISH WITH RED LIPS 106

COLOURFUL HERONS 107

PARAKEETS THAT CAN SURVIVE A MONTH WITHOUT WATER 108

THE STRUCTURE OF BIRDS' FEATHERS 110

BIRDS' TECHNIQUES OF SOARING 114

THE WATER BIRD THAT CUTS THROUGH THE WATER LIKE SCISSORS 116

CUTTLEFISH LIKE JET ENGINES 119

GREYLAG GEESE 120

A MATCHLESS SECURITY SYSTEM 122

CONCLUSION 125

WONDERFUL CREATURES

INTRODUCTION

There are innumerable kinds of living creatures on the face of the earth. From pets such as cats, which we come across everyday, to animals inhabiting virgin forests, every species has wondrous features and amazing skills. For example we are surprised to see how bees can build such perfect honeycombs and can do calculations as if they were expert mathematicians. As we see how considerate a crocodile or a lion is to its young, we wonder how such wild animals can behave so affectionately. We seek an answer to the question how can little birds, which cover thousands of kilometres during a non-stop migration, perform this hard task. The more detailed information we get, the more amazed we become.

Every living being has a particular body structure. Some fly, others swim. For example the body structure of a fish is exactly as it needs for life underwater. It has the lungs, eyes and skin that enable it to live underwater. The lungs and feathers of birds have the structures that enable them to fly. There is no doubt that these living creatures did not by themselves obtain the skills or body structures with which they carry out extraordinary tasks. These creatures are not the ones who invented the tasks, each of which is more astonishing than another. They could not possibly have learnt the tasks they carry out by chance either. It is not possible for them to know all these things unless there is someone who taught them everything they do. Besides, there should be someone who designed the structure they needed and placed it in their bodies. There is a Being Who is exalted in power and intelligence. This being is our Lord, Who created us as well as all other living creatures. Allah gave all the features they possess.

You may already know these facts, however there are some people who claim the opposite. Did you know that these people claim that living creatures obtained all the wonderful features they have by chance? And have you heard that they named these nonsensical claims "the theory of evolution"? Moreover, even though all branches of science have revealed the fallacy of the claims of the theory of evolution, these people do not give up maintaining this senseless claim.

In this book, we will examine the wondrous features of living creatures. By giving examples of the claims of evolutionists, we will also show how senseless the theory is. As you read the book, you will be surprised to see how mistaken professors, engineers and scientists who believe in the theory of evolution could be. (For further information about evolutionists see

WONDERFUL CREATURES

Wonders of Allah's Creation by Harun Yahya, Taha Publishers, London, 2002.)

In fact, factual information about living creatures is too abundant to be collected even in volumes of books. For this reason only some examples will be examined in this book. Yet, even with these few examples, you will be able to better comprehend the greatness of Allah, Who created these pretty creatures for us, and how much He loves us. You will reflect on what you'll learn and will be eager to tell it to others.

He is Allah – the Creator, the Maker, the Giver of Form. To Him belong the Most Beautiful Names. Everything in the heavens and earth glorifies Him. He is the Almighty, the All-Wise. (Surat al-Hashr: 24)

WONDERFUL CREATURES

BLIND TERMITES BUILDING SKYSCRAPERS

Termites are as small insects as ants, and they are very skilful. The nests in these pictures that look like tall towers are built by these little creatures. But make no mistake: these are not simple nests; termites build them according to a plan. Special chambers for the young, fungus production fields and the queen's chamber are only a few of the sections in a termite nest. More importantly, there is a special ventilation system. Termites, whose skins are very thin, need humid air. For that reason they need to keep the temperature and humidity of the nest at a certain level. Otherwise termites would die. They make the air circulate through

the nest by means of special channels and use the water that comes from underground tunnels they have dug, and thus regulate the temperature and humidity.

Have you realised how hard this process is, and that termites have to act in a way marked by careful consideration of many things together? Besides that, what we have mentioned so far is merely a brief summary of the numerous things that termites do.

Another characteristic of termites is their defence of the nest, which may be up to seven metres. Termites are alarmed whenever there is a hole in the walls of their nest. Hitting their heads against the walls, termites on watch give warning to all members of the colony. Upon this warning, larvae are moved to securer places. The entrances of the chamber where the king and the queen live are blocked by quickly built walls. The damaged section is surrounded by soldier termites, which are followed by workers who carry the material to restore the wall. In a few hours, the destroyed area is covered with a heap. Then the inner compartments are constructed. Termites act following a prescribed plan and each member of the colony carries out its task without causing any disorder.

That they can do all these things in quite a short time is evidence of perfect communication between termites. Yet there is something even more amazing about the termites that establish such order, build colonies like sky-scrapers and take security precautions to protect their colonies: they are BLIND.

They see nothing while carrying out all these tasks. How can these creatures be so skilful and make such plans?

The answer that evolutionists provide to such questions is that they happen "by chance". However this answer is not correct. That is because even a single part of the order in a termite colony, say the ventilation channels, is sufficient to prove that such a system cannot come into existence by chance. No doubt blind termites cannot ensure this perfect order and cannot have all the work performed so faultlessly. Obviously they are taught what to do.

Allah has mentioned some animals in the Qur'an and urged us to reflect on these examples. For instance, the honeybee is given as an example in Surat an-Nahl. We are informed in the verse that bees that produce honey for us are taught what to do by our Lord. The verses are:

Your Lord revealed to the bees: "Build dwellings in the mountains and the trees, and also in the structures which men erect. Then eat from every kind of fruit and travel the paths of your Lord, which have been made easy for you to follow." From inside them comes a drink of varying

colours, containing healing for mankind. There is certainly a Sign in that for people who reflect. *(Surat an-Nahl: 68-69)*

Just like the bees referred to in the above verses, termites live in the way Allah teaches them and reveals to them. It is our Lord Who creates perfect communication between these sightless creatures, teaches them what to do and makes each one of the millions of termites in a colony perform its task.

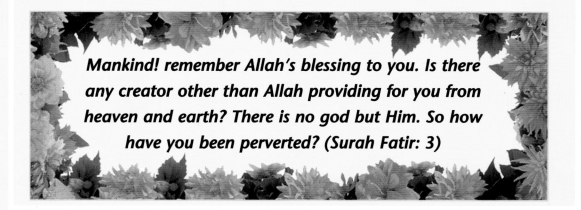

Mankind! remember Allah's blessing to you. Is there any creator other than Allah providing for you from heaven and earth? There is no god but Him. So how have you been perverted? *(Surah Fatir: 3)*

WONDERFUL CREATURES

SECURITY MEASURES OF ANIMALS

It is among the miracles in nature that living creatures take precautions to protect themselves. Many creatures have the capability to estimate potential hazards and to invent various security methods. For instance, the termites that we mentioned build the walls of their colonies so thick and hard that they can hardly be destroyed even with a pickaxe. Weaverbirds build the entrance of their nests in such a way as to prevent snakes, their main enemies, from entering. Some spiders have special chambers in their nests in which other animals that have somehow entered the nest are confined.

Beehives also operate special protective measures. The bees that are employed to stand guard over the hive do not let anyone in other than members of the colony. When a guardian is away, another worker bee comes to the entrance of the hive and

The birds in the pictures build nests so as to prevent their enemies from entering. Termite nests, such as the tower-like one to the side and the mushroom-like one above, are as strong as castles.

WONDERFUL CREATURES

Building their dams in streams, beavers stop the flow of water and construct wonderful lodges for themselves.

takes over the watch. Moreover these guardian bees carry out this task at the risk of their own lives.

Beavers build their lodges underwater. In order to enter, one has to pass through a secret tunnel known only by the beaver that built that lodge. At the end of the tunnel, there is a chamber where beavers live together with their offspring.

Even these examples are sufficient for us to understand that there is intelligence in the way living creatures act and that they employ very effective methods to protect themselves. Besides, you may have noted that the enemy of a species may be another species. However, all creatures know their enemies very well and take elaborate precautions against them. It is quite surprising that a termite or a bird, despite the fact that it lacks advanced intellectual functions, can know the features of another creature.

To comprehend it better, think about yourself. Can you understand at first sight the characteristics of an animal that you do not know and have not seen before? Can you know what it feeds on, how it hunts and what it fears? Of course you cannot. You need a book to read and to get information about that creature or someone to tell you about its attributes. But how can animals have information about other creatures? Might they have found out who their enemies are and then conducted a study of their behaviour and hunting methods, upon the basis of which they have developed suitable precautions? Certainly not. No animal has the intellectual capabilities and talent to do research. Besides, it would also be unreason-

able and nonsensical to think that animals gathered information about their enemies by chance, because failing in the first attempt would mean death.

Undoubtedly it is Allah Who determines the security measures that animals use and makes them act as necessary. The fact that not only the animals we see around us, but all living creatures in the world behave in the same intelligent way points to the infinite wisdom and power of our Lord.

COMPASS IN THE ANT'S EYE

We need guides to show us the direction when we travel to another country or another city. In particular, when we do not know the place we are going to, we definitely must have a compass and a map. Map shows us where we are and the compass shows us which way to go. We find the way by using these tools and consulting other people so we do not get lost. Have you ever wondered how other creatures find their way? Have you ever thought how an ant seeking food in the desert returns to its nest?

Black desert ants inhabiting the Mediterranean coasts of Tunisia are among those creatures who build their nests in the desert. These ants are very good at finding their way in the vast desert and getting back to their nests without the help of a compass or a map.

As the sun rises, temperatures in the desert reach up to 70ºC (158ºF). The ant leaves its nest to find food in the heat of the day. Frequently halting and turning around itself, it follows a devious route within an area that may be 200 metres (655 feet) away from the nest. You may see this route on the map. But do not think that the ant will get lost because of these zig-zags. Once it finds a source of food, the ant follows a straight course and

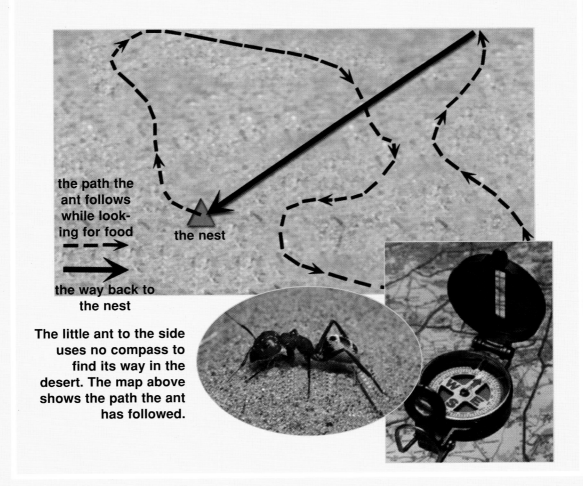

the path the ant follows while looking for food

– – – ➔

➔

the way back to the nest

the nest

The little ant to the side uses no compass to find its way in the desert. The map above shows the path the ant has followed.

returns to the nest. With respect to their sizes, this journey of the ant may be compared to a man's returning to his starting point taking a straight course after wandering 35-40 kilometres (22-25 miles) away from that point in the desert. How is it that an ant successfully does a task that is virtually impossible for a human?

It cannot be that the ant finds its direction by looking at objects. Signs and way-marks such as trees, rocks, rivers or lakes which help one find the way are quite rare in the desert. There is only sand all around. Even if there were such signs, it would not make any difference since it is not possible for an ant to keep these signs in mind, to memorise where they are and to use them while finding its way. Thinking about it this way, one can better understand the significance of the task that the ant performs. The ant can perform this difficult task thanks to the special body structure it has been given.

There is a special direction-determination system in the ant's eyes. This system that Allah placed in the ant's eyes is more advanced than mechanical devices that determine direction. Being able to perceive some rays that we cannot, the ant can determine directions and know where north and south are. Thanks to this ability, it is not difficult at all for the ant to estimate where its nest is and to return to it.

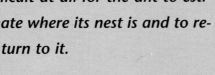

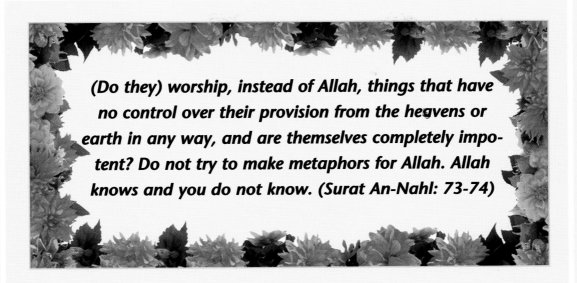

(Do they) worship, instead of Allah, things that have no control over their provision from the heavens or earth in any way, and are themselves completely impotent? Do not try to make metaphors for Allah. Allah knows and you do not know. (Surat An-Nahl: 73-74)

Human beings have lately become aware of the characteristics of light. However the ant has known and used a characteristic of light, which was unknown to human beings, since it was born. Certainly such a perfect structure as the eye of this ant cannot be attributed to random coincidences. The eyes of the ant must have been so since it came into existence. Otherwise the ant could not return to the nest in the desert heat and could not survive. Indeed, eyes of all desert ants have been equipped with this system since the first day they came into existence. Allah, the All-Knowing, created these eyes for them.

THE MARVELLOUS CO-OPERATION OF THE ANT AND THE BIRD

There are microbes everywhere that threaten our health and cause diseases. These microbes are a danger to other living creatures as well as human beings. Therefore these creatures, too, need to protect themselves just as we do. When living creatures are observed, we see that they use some methods to protect themselves against microbes. For instance, ants produce a kind of acidic substance that incapacitates microbes. They apply this acidic substance to their bodies and to the walls of their nest. In other words, they know that not only they themselves but also the nest they live in should be purified of microbes.

How is it that a little ant can know to act so intelligently? No doubt the ant's intellectual power is not enough for that. An ant can know neither what a microbe is nor that it should protect itself from it. The ant should have first analysed the microbe and then found the substance to render it harmless. But how could it have determined this substance?

Let's think together.

People are inoculated against specific microbes, but these vaccines are prepared in laboratories as a result of much research and experiment.

Ants, which are very tiny creatures, are aware that microbes are harmful to them and take the appropriate precautions. They produce a kind of acid that deactivates microbes. Allah inspires ants to do this.

Moreover, experts perform this research, for otherwise the vaccine would not be of any use, and could even be harmful. Ants, on the other hand, do not have such knowledge and have not been trained. They cannot possibly go to a laboratory and do research. It is unreasonable even to think such a thing. Obviously ants are born into the world knowing all these things that they do.

This knowledge is taught to the ant by a superior Being: Allah, the Lord of all the worlds and the Creator of everything, reveals to the ant how to protect itself from microbes.

Now let's take birds as another example of living creatures that should be protected against microbes. Microbes disturb birds too, but birds do not have a system in their bodies to produce protective substances as ants do. Consequently birds have found a different but equally practical solution to this problem. They go to and lie upon an ant's nest, and wait for the ants to wander through their feathers. Ants that search for food stroll among the bird's feathers and the substance that kills the microbes is smeared on the bird's feathers as they do so. Thus, the bird is purified of microbes. How do birds know that ants produce such a substance and that this substance will remove microbes from their bodies?

People have discovered that ants have such a protective system only after much research. Many people other than those who have expert knowledge about animals are still not aware of it. Probably you too, have just learnt about it here. Birds, however, have known this feature of ants from the moment they were born. Moreover,

WONDERFUL CREATURES

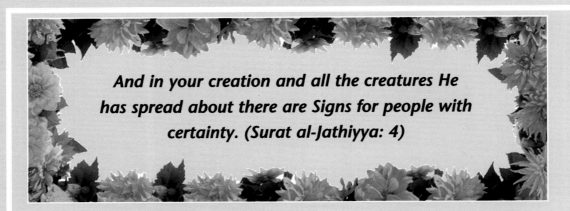

And in your creation and all the creatures He has spread about there are Signs for people with certainty. (Surat al-Jathiyya: 4)

although there is nobody to teach them how to do it, they can use ants to be cleansed of microbes.

The fact that birds can know about a substance produced in an ant's body and can know how to make use of it leads us to a single fact: Allah teaches this information to both creatures. Allah has revealed that every being is under His command :

... No, everything in the heavens and earth belongs to Him. Everything is obedient to Him. (Surat al-Baqara: 116)

LITTLE ENGINEERING BIRDS

You certainly must have seen birds' nests built on trees or on tops of buildings, and sometimes on a corner of a balcony. These are merely the nests of the few bird species that you know. But so many bird species live in the world and they build so many different types of nests that one should really reflect on this.

Before all other considerations, birds build their nests so that they blend in with their natural environments. Let us consider birds of the shoreline. These birds build their nests on the surface of the water and the nest does not sink. The materials used and the shape of the nest are all particularly designed. So, even if the water level rises, neither the nest nor the offspring are damaged. These animals have innate capabilities to build their nests and have no need of training. They could not have possibly learnt such a task over time; if they had tried to do it by trial and error, the nest would have sunk as the water rose. However such a thing never happens because all shoreline birds have built their nests in the same way since the first day they appeared.

Some birds living in swamps build the walls of their nests high so that the eggs do not fall out because of the wind. How is it that this bird, which carefully protects its egg, knows about the risk of eggs falling out and being broken? We see here that the bird takes a wise precaution.

WONDERFUL CREATURES

WONDERFUL CREATURES

Another bird species living in arid areas builds its nest among the bushes and not on the ground. The reason why it does so is the difference in temperature: the temperature among the bushes is ten degrees less than on the ground. Most of us do not know about the temperature difference between the ground and bushes, and that there is a difference between them. These birds, however, know it and protect themselves and their young from intense heat by building their nest in the coolest place.

Birds build their nests in safe places especially chosen by them.

Have you ever wondered how birds, which lack consciousness and intellect as we understand them, can consider such delicate details?

These behaviours of birds could be compared to those of engineers who have gone through years of education and training in their fields. While building a house, engineers consider details such as the strength of the building, materials to be used and location; only then can construction begin. As you have seen in the above examples, birds also build their nests according to a plan. But they do not need any tools or education. They act by the inspiration of Allah and carry out their tasks easily. These birds and what they perform are evidence of Allah's perfect creation. It is surely the All-Knowing Allah Who inspires them to do everything they do.

Everything in the heavens and everything in the earth belongs to Him. Allah is the Rich Beyond Need, the Praiseworthy. (Surat al-Hajj: 64)

WONDERFUL CREATURES

THE HEATING SYSTEM OF THE WINTER MOTH

When winter comes, many insect species inhabiting cold regions of the world die from cold or lack of food. That is because insects are delicate creatures, but there are some exceptions to this rule. For example, owl moths look like butterflies and at first sight seem very delicate. In reality, however, they are strong enough to survive tough winter conditions. Therefore these moths are also called "winter moths".

Like butterflies, a winter moth has two wings and a trunk to which these wings are joined. In order for this moth to fly, the temperature of its thorax to which its wings are affixed should be 30°C (86°F). But the temperature where they live is usually 0°C (32°F) and even drops below minus degrees from time to time. How could winter moths survive such cold? What prevents them from freezing when they are motionless and what enables them to fly in cold weather?

This moth species is created together with a special heating system that enables it to live under winter conditions. This system consists of several complementary features.

Before flight winter moths continuously tense the main muscles that are connected to the wings and make their wings quiver. The rapid quivering of the wings leads to an increase in the temperature of the insect's thorax. Thanks to this increase, the temperature of the thorax may rise from 0°C (32°F) to 30°C (86°F) or even more. However, this is only one of the features that the moth needs to survive. In order to fly it is not sufficient for the winter moth merely to increase its body temperature. That is because the difference between the temperatures of the insect's body and of the atmosphere will result in loss of heat. In the same way as a glass of hot tea cools after a while, the moth's body will also cool. Therefore it will not help even if the moth keeps its wings quivering. In order for the winter moth to fly and thus to live, another method is required to maintain the heat it has produced. This need is also met by a special structure that Allah created in the moth's body. Moths are covered with dense scales that reduce heat loss. Scientists have determined after research that a moth without scales cools twice as fast as those with scales.

These are some of the mechanisms in a winter moth that protect it from cold. The features mentioned above must have existed since this moth species came into being. Otherwise, the moth would die of cold and this species would be extinct. One does not need to reflect at great length to understand that it is not a coincidence that only those species inhabiting cold regions possess these features that make them different from all other moths. Taking all kinds of measures to enable these creatures to survive in cold, Allah introduces Himself to us. It is related in a verse that Allah knows where all creatures live:

There is no creature on the earth which is not dependent upon Allah for its provision. He knows where it lives and where it dies. They are all in a Clear Book. (Surah Hud: 6)

Such features in living creatures enable us to grasp Allah's power and artistry, and increase our faith in and love for our Lord. Communicating the amazing information you read to others, you may also be the means to increase other people's faith in Allah.

HOW DO SALMON FIND THEIR WAY?

You are mistaken if you think that migration is peculiar to birds. In fact, there are many migratory species on land and in sea. In this section, the adventure of salmon, a migratory fish species, will be examined.

Salmon are born into the world as they hatch from eggs the females of the species lay in the river. They grow and hunt in this place for several weeks after which they start to advance down the river. During this journey towards the sea, they encounter dams and polluted water, and try to avoid dangers such as bigger hunting fishes. Having overcome all these and reached the sea, they spend several years there. Once they mature enough to spawn, they swim back to the fresh water.

WONDERFUL CREATURES

WONDERFUL CREATURES

The point at which salmon aim to arrive is the place they were born. But make no mistake: it's not a short distance. The distance that the fish needs to cover to get to the destination may sometimes be 1,500 km (930 miles), which means a demanding journey of months. There are many obstacles that the fish has to overcome during this journey.

The first, and maybe the most important problem that needs to be solved is to find where the river down which the fish swam during its first journey empties into the sea. Based on this, the fish will determine the return route to follow. Amazingly, none of the salmon makes a mistake and they all find the river right first time.

Entering the stream, the salmon starts to steadfastly swim against the current. This time its task is harder because, whereas it could easily pass down waterfalls with the assistance of the current the first time, it has to climb up over them this time. What the salmon in this picture intends by leaping upriver is to reach the place where it was spawned. During this journey the salmon may need to swim through shallow waters that leave its upper fin above water. These shallow waters are full of birds, bears and many wild predators.

The difficulties that the salmon has to overcome are not limited to these. Recall that it hatched from the egg in a branch of a river, in a *quite inner part of the land. In order to reach that point, it has to go the correct way when the river forks into branches. Salmon do not make any mistake in these choices and they always follow the correct stream.*

Now suppose that you were born and had grown up in a house in a city. Then one day you left your house, travelled for days and came to a place 1,500 km (930 miles) away from home. Years passed and you desired to return to your place of birth. Do you think that you could possibly remember streets that you passed only once? While no human being could, salmon can and they always find their way faultlessly.

There have been various studies to understand how salmon make this exceptional journey. It has been concluded that salmon find their way by use of "smell".

Thanks to its ingeniously structured nose, a salmon can pursue a scent in the water to its source just as a hound does. In fact, every current has a distinctive smell. The young salmon records all the smells during its journey and returns home by recalling these smells.

How does this extraordinary thing happen? How could every salmon find its way correctly? Why do all salmon try to return to their place of birth, risking their lives, leaping waterfalls and confronting wild animals? What is more, they do not do all these things for themselves but simply in order to deposit their eggs in these waters.

There is only one answer to these questions: Allah, the All-Knowing, cre-

ated the salmon and the systems that enable them to find their way. Like all creatures, salmon act by the inspiration they receive from Allah and they manifest the Lord's excellent creation.

Among the evidence that refutes the theory of evolution is that salmon cover thousands of kilometres and risk their own lives to spawn.

Evolutionists claim that all creatures are always in a struggle with each other and that only the strong survive at the end of this struggle. However, there is a co-operation among living creatures contrary to evolutionists' assertions. Animals risk their own lives for their offspring. Besides, as you will see in the examples given in the following pages, there are different species that associate with and benefit each other. The salmon is merely one of the creatures that display self-sacrificing behaviour for their offspring. Salmon that migrate and manage to reach the place to spawn, which are very small in number, will die soon after they produce their spawn. Yet they never give up their journey. Such self-sacrificing behavioural patterns cannot by any means be explained by the theory of evolution. The fact is evident. Allah created salmon and these creatures behave in the way that Allah inspires in them. People who use their intellect take lessons from such behaviour of animals. Allah reminds us to do so in a verse :

There is no creature He does not hold by the forelock... (Surah Hud: 56)

WONDERFUL CREATURES

HOW DO FISH LIVE IN WATER?

You must have seen how fast and brisk fish are in water. In order to swim, a fish does not need to make any movement other than to wag its tail from side to side. This ease of movement that fish have in water is thanks to their flexible backbones as well as some systems in their bodies.

A fish expends a large amount of energy while swimming. This is not because it swims fast for long times. Fish need considerable amounts of energy in order to reach high speeds from being still. It is vital for a fish to gain speed instantaneously because it needs to do so in order to escape from predators.

Moreover, fish move against the current most of the time. Consider how hard it is for you to move in water and how easy it is to move while you are walking in the street. Compare living underwater and living on the face of earth.

It is the special structure of the backbone and muscles of the fish that provide it such power. The backbone keeps the body straight and is connected to the fins and muscles. Otherwise, it would not be possible for the fish to move in the water. However, the particular shape of the backbone is not sufficient to enable the act of swimming. That is because fish not only move forward and backward, but also upward and downward in order to survive. This movement is made possible by another system in their bodies. Fish have air sacs in their bodies. By emptying these sacs of air, fish can sink to the bottom of the sea, and

In the creation of the heavens and earth, and the alternation of the night and day, and the ships which sail the seas to people's benefit, and the water which Allah sends down from the sky – by which He brings the earth to life when it was dead and scatters about in it creatures of every kind – and the varying direction of the winds, and the clouds subservient between heaven and earth, there are Signs for people who use their intellect. (Surat al-Baqara: 164)

by filling the sacs with air fish can rise to the surface again.

Have you ever wondered how fish are not damaged at all although they are always in the water? Our skin becomes affected if we stay in water for a while; if we stay for a longer time then our skin be-

comes injured. But this never happens to a fish. This is thanks to a stiff bright layer in its outer skin. This layer prevents water from entering its body. If fish did not have this layer, their bodies would be damaged, and since water would enter the body the balance would be disturbed and they would eventually die. However, these do not happen and all fish continue to live their underwater lives.

All fish species in the world possess these features. Species that lived long ago possessed them too. Fish have had the same perfect structure for millions of years and have not gone through any change. It is possible to see this in the remnants of fish that lived millions of years ago. These remnants, namely fossils, clearly reveal that fish were the same as they are today and have not changed at all. This is evidence that fish came into existence at one point in time. In other words, they were created. It is Allah Who gave fish all the features they have and Who created everything in the universe. He knows the needs of all creatures.

The picture on the left shows the remains, in other words a fossil, of a fish that lived a very long time ago. Another member of the same species, one that is still alive today, can be seen in the picture below. As you can see, there is no difference between the two.

WONDERFUL CREATURES

HOW DO MACAWS KNOW CHEMISTRY?

Some plants have poisonous seeds. This is an effective method of protection against their enemies who try to eat them. Yet a parrot species living in America can feed on these poisonous seeds. This is quite surprising because while other creatures cannot approach the seeds, these birds that continually eat them are not affected at all. You are curious about how this happens, aren't you?

How this parrot species called the macaw is not poisoned has attracted the attention of scientists too. Scientists observed macaws and witnessed a quite extraordinary pattern of behaviour.

Having eaten these nutritious but poisonous seeds, macaws fly towards a rocky place. There they gnaw upon and swallow some clay containing rocks. This is not a random behaviour. Indeed, rocks that contain clay absorb the poison of the seeds. This is how the macaw can digest the seeds without suffering.

How has this bird acquired the medical knowledge to diagnose the poisonous effect of the seed? How does it know how to get rid of this poisonous

You have read in this book that macaws feed on rocks that contain clay, as seen in the picture. If you had seen this picture before reading this book, the behaviour of this parrot species would have surprised you. Maybe you would not even have understood what they were doing. But now you know why macaws eat clay. Most importantly, you know that Allah teaches them to do so. Tell others about what you have learnt to enhance their faith in Allah as well.

effect? Could it possibly have had an education in pharmacy to know that a substance that neutralises the effects of the poison is available in rocks that contain clay? Of course not.

A human being could not understand whether a seed is poisonous or not by its appearance. He could not estimate how to neutralise the effects of the poison. In order to be able to do that, he would have needed education or to have consulted those with knowledge. This being the case, it cannot be claimed that a bird with no intellectual faculties might have discovered such a thing after long chemical analyses and study. It is not possible for macaws to acquire this knowledge, which can be learnt by human beings only after years of special education, by chance. All-Knowing Allah, Who creates everything perfectly, teaches macaws this knowledge.

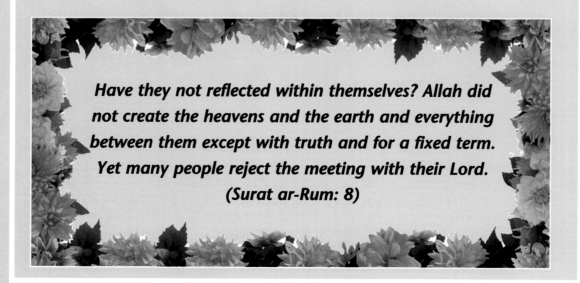

Have they not reflected within themselves? Allah did not create the heavens and the earth and everything between them except with truth and for a fixed term. Yet many people reject the meeting with their Lord. (Surat ar-Rum: 8)

ENGINEERING IN THE COBWEB

Have you ever noticed the shapes of spider webs? Did you know that spiders produce their thread themselves and that this thread has some amazing characteristics? Or have you heard that the techniques used by garden spiders to spin a web are the same as those used by civil engineers today?

A spider needs two separate places in order to spin its web. Webs are generally spun in a corner where two walls join or between two branches. However, some spiders are so skilful that they spin their web using a single surface. How a spider spins its web is spectacular. Now try to visualise what we will tell you here.

A spider first finds a flexible branch that is long enough to spin its web. It firmly fastens a thread to the end of the branch. Walking down the branch, it continues to secrete thread. Once it covers a certain distance, it stops and ceases to secrete. It pulls the thread it has secreted until the branch is bent like a bow. The spider sticks the other end of the thread, which is now as straight as a string, firmly to that point. Then it starts to spin its web inside this bow.

Now consider what you would do if you were to stretch a string two and a half metres long between two walls that are two metres apart from each

WONDERFUL CREATURES

other. While you are trying to find out how, let us explain how a species of garden spider has solved this problem.

Garden spiders sometimes spin their web between two distant branches. Since such webs are quite large, they have a high capacity to catch prey. Nevertheless, their large size results in a gradual decrease in the tautness of the web, which means a decrease in the ability to catch prey. So spiders need a solution. You might have thought that the spider would spin a new web once the web is not taut enough any more. But instead of replacing the web the spider does something amazing: It secretes a thread from the centre of the web down to the ground, and fixes a small stone on to that end of the thread which is close to ground. Returning to the web and pulling the thread, it lifts the stone. Then it fastens the thread, at one end of which the stone swings in the air, once again on the centre of the web. Consequently, the web is taut again as the weight of the stone hanging from the web stretches it down.

You would probably not come up with such a solution neither would many people who do not have knowledge of construction. However spiders know and apply this technique. How does a spider know such an admirable technique and apply it so well? Moreover, every spider has spun its web applying the same technique for millions of years. There needs to be an "Authority" Who inspires the

WONDERFUL CREATURES

spider to use this technique because the authority to do it does not belong to the spider itself. This power belongs to the Almighty Allah, Possessor of everything, Who guides and inspires all living creatures with what they should do.

AN INTERESTING CREATURE: NAUTILUS

You must have seen submarines on TV or in journals. These vessels, which are capable of operating far below the surface of the sea without being noticed, are used in ensuring national security and in some scientific research. How submarines operate is: As the special diving tanks in a submarine are filled with water, the vessel becomes heavier than water and sinks deep down in the ocean. If water in the tank is emptied and replaced by pressurised air, the submarine rises up to the surface of the water again.

Now we will examine the nautilus, a very interesting creature that employs exactly the same method. The nautilus has a spiral, pearly-lines shell and dives as submarines do. It has an organ shaped like a snail shell that is 19 cm (7,5 inch) in diameter, as shown in the picture. This organ contains twenty-eight interconnected "diving chambers". These diving cham-

bers operate in the same way as the tanks in a submarine do; in other words the nautilus needs pressurised air. In submarines, this need is met by a special system established by engineers in relevant places in the submarine. But how does the nautilus find the pressurised air necessary to expel the water?

The answer to this question introduces us to another amazing feature that Allah created. A special gas is produced in the nautilus' body. This gas is conveyed to the chambers through its bloodstream and eventually expels the water from the cells. So a nautilus can sink or float to protect itself against its enemies while hunting. In fact the diving capacity of the nautilus is much higher than that of a submarine. A submarine dives only to 400 metres (1310 feet) while it is so easy for a nautilus to dive to 4,000 metres (2,5 miles).

You have noticed that there is no difference between the fossil of a nautilus that lived a long time ago (below) and the nautilus of our day, haven't you?

WONDERFUL CREATURES

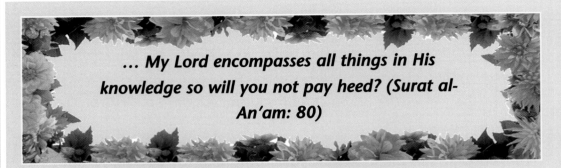

... My Lord encompasses all things in His knowledge so will you not pay heed? (Surat al-An'am: 80)

The special system of this interesting marine animal is created for us to reflect on it. Now consider for a moment. Could a nautilus have attained this system by chance? Could it itself have acquired the bodily structure that enables gas production? Furthermore, this is not the only feature of the nautilus. The pressure underwater is quite intense. This is why you feel pressure in your ears when you dive deep. Nevertheless the pressure you experience is comparatively low; as one descends further in the water, the pressure increases and after a certain depth has deadly effects on living creatures. However, although it is a very small being and has only an external shell to protect itself, the nautilus is not affected by this pressure, which can be extreme.

Obviously, all features that a nautilus has are designed. This being cannot possibly on its own design the bodily structure to resist a pressure of tons underwater. Allah, Who originates everything perfectly, designed this excellent structure. In a verse of the Qur'an, Allah invites people to be heedful:

Is He Who creates like him who does not create? So will you not pay heed? (Surat An-Nahl: 17)

BUTTERFLIES THAT HAVE KNOWLEDGE OF PHYSICS

The appearance of butterflies is admirable. These creatures, which with their colourful wings and elegant flight are like living ornaments, are some of the sources of beauty that Allah creates for us. However, a marvellous appearance is certainly not the only feature of butterflies. These short-lived creatures sometimes do calculations such as a specialist would do. For example, like the moths which we discussed earlier, the body heat of a butterfly should be at a certain temperature in order for it to fly. Let's see what butterflies do to solve this problem.

The colias butterfly cannot fly when its body temperature is below 28°C (83°F). In such cases the butterfly opens its wings to expose its upper side to the sun and to soak up the sun's rays at the correct angle. If its body temperature rises as high as 40°C (104°F), it rotates by 90 degrees and thus receives the sun's rays horizontally. With this behaviour the butterfly absorbs as little heat through the wings as possible and its body temperature decreases.

Besides that, this butterfly species has little dark spots on its wings. These spots, the function of which is to maintain a higher body temperature, are not located in an

unspecified place. They are close to the points that are most needed to be warm. Thanks to this particular design, heat transmission from these spots, which warm quickly, to other parts of the body is facilitated since the distance that needs to be covered to transmit heat is shortened.

Another butterfly species employs a similar method to increase its body temperature. You all know what a lens is. Some are used to produce enlarged images whereas some others are used to produce smaller images of objects. For example glasses consist of a pair of lenses. Besides this function, a lens angled correctly toward the sun can concentrate the sun's rays on a certain spot. Using this method it is possible even to light a fire. The pieris, another butterfly species, angle its wings toward the sun so that all rays are concentrated on certain parts of its body that need most to warm, in a similar way as a lens functions.

Certainly these butterflies have not had an education in physics or in any other field. They cannot know about the features of a lens. They do not know which angle would receive the greatest amount of heat. Allah, Who watches over and protects all things, inspires in butterflies what they should do to regulate their body temperature. As Allah reminds us in a verse:

... Allah is watchful over all things. (Surat al-Ahzab: 52)

MALE CATFISH ON DUTY

It is not generally known that fish build nests and provide continuous protection for their offspring. These nests are generally holes dug among pebbles or in the sand. Eggs develop in these open nests for some time, during which the mother and father fish take turns to keep watch over the nest for enemies.

Catfish are among these creatures that protect their young. Female catfish spawn eggs at the bottom of plants and reeds in shallow water. Eggs cling to the roots of these plants. After a while, the female leaves her eggs and then it is the male's turn to take on the duty. The male's duty is to stay with the eggs and to keep watch for danger. This sentry duty lasts for about 40-50 days after which the young fish become fully mature.

WONDERFUL CREATURES

Besides this vigilance, the male also makes a murmuring sound using his gills and in this way keeps other hostile fish away from the eggs. He knows that this sound will threaten other fish and will force them to go away.

Allah inspires male catfish to protect their young in this way. Like all creatures, this fish acts only in the way that Allah inspires in it and thus ensures the continuance of its species.

DID YOU KNOW ABOUT LUMINESCENT CREATURES?

Have you ever seen lights moving in trees at night? The source of these lights, which may sometimes be so many that a tree may be suffused with them all over, is fireflies. Fireflies are the best known of luminescent living creatures. These creatures, which emit light and illuminate trees in the darkness of the night, are among those that scientists have studied most. Soon we will examine why, but first let's see how these creatures use light.

Fireflies produce green-yellow lights in their bodies. Light is the means of communication for fireflies. As well as giving mating signals, this light is also used for defence from enemies. By means of light, their enemies understand that fireflies are not tasty and thus decide not to feed on them.

The main characteristic of these beetles is that they make the most of light and they virtually

WONDERFUL CREATURES

Scientists have tried for years to imitate the light that fireflies emit, yet have not been successful. This is among the evidence that Allah created fireflies with a perfect design.

do not waste any energy. Therefore fireflies have become a subject for investigation by scientists for years. However, despite all the research that has been carried out, humans have not yet produced a light as prolific as that of fireflies.

It is amazing how a living creature produces light, yet is not adversely affected by its heat. You must have noticed that lamps produce heat as well as illumination. If you touch a source of light, for example, a light bulb, the heat burns your hand. So you might wonder how the firefly is not injured by the heat it produces. In fact, that's what is so amazing about luminescent creatures: the heat they produce does not affect them. That is because the light produced by these creatures is completely different from what we use as a medium of illumination. This light is called "cold light", and heat is not emitted during the production of this type of light. Therefore production of this type of light is very effective and scientists have tried for years to imitate this type of light.

As well as fireflies, various underwater creatures, insects and other species also produce their own light. Each has a different way to produce its light, different fields in which to use the light and different durations and types of light. And each on its own is a wonder.

Obviously, it was not the creatures who equipped themselves with the systems to produce light and who ensure the continuance of these systems. A system that produces light in a living creature's body cannot possibly come into existence as a result of coincidences. Moreover, a structure so perfect

The creatures seen in the pictures live in the dark depths of the sea thanks to the luminescent quality that Allah has given to them.

that does not cause any damage to the body could not have possibly emerged during the production process. All luminescent creatures are evidence of Allah's artistry in excellent creation. Allah shows us the evidence of His eternal knowledge, intelligence and power in the creatures He creates. He also reminds mankind that no matter how hard man tries, he cannot bring the flawless mechanisms in nature into existence unless our Lord wills.

LUMINESCENT UNDERWATER CREATURES

Many underwater creatures, like the ones shown in the pictures, possess systems as fireflies do for producing light. They generally use their light to stupefy or frighten their enemies. Almost all of them have series of cells along their backs like seams of a fabric and these cells can produce light. Now let's have a look at the general characteristics of these creatures.

One of these species is an animal that looks like a jellyfish. They generally feed on small marine animals and plants that are invisible to the naked eye. Some seize their prey by use of their sticky tentacles, which move in water like a fishing line. Members of another species have such large mouths that they can open them wide and swallow many creatures. They have series of thin hairs on their bodies, which they use to propel themselves forward in the water.

Luminescent creatures have some other extraordinary traits. For example, some red species shine when they are struck, and can leave glitteringly illuminated particles in the water. This is a way to confuse, and thus to escape from, their enemies.

Creatures like starfish, sea urchins and feather stars are "spiny": Many of these creatures are covered with spines, which are used as a means of defence. They live on seashores, in coral reefs and on the seabed. These creatures also produce their own light to protect themselves against their enemies. Having luminous arms or spines, they can also produce clouds of light in the water when they are attacked.

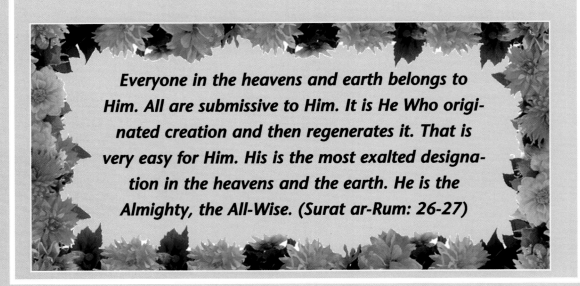

Everyone in the heavens and earth belongs to Him. All are submissive to Him. It is He Who originated creation and then regenerates it. That is very easy for Him. His is the most exalted designation in the heavens and the earth. He is the Almighty, the All-Wise. (Surat ar-Rum: 26-27)

The most interesting feature of luminescent marine creatures is probably the fact that they use their light to mislead others. A starfish species is a good example of this. This starfish species lives about 1,000 metres (3,280 feet) deep in the sea. It emits bright green-blue light from the tip of its arms. This gleaming warning notifies its enemies that it is not tasty. Another starfish species starts flashing when it is attacked and detaches and throws one of its arms towards the enemy to divert it. The attention of its enemy is distracted by the torn arm, which still emits white light. In the meantime the starfish finds the time to flee.

As we have seen in the few examples given above, the mechanisms in living creatures that enable them to produce light demonstrate to us the perfect creation of Allah. What have been mentioned here are creatures that live underwater, the dominant component of whose bodies is usually water – as in our own bodies – and that cannot possibly have intelligence like that of human beings. Yet each possesses such wonderful features that it astonishes us to know about them. This reveals that Allah originates things matchlessly. These examples are in order to make us comprehend that there is no other god besides Allah, the Creator of everything. One who under-

stands this will comprehend Allah's infinite might and will strive only to earn Allah's good pleasure.

Remember that Allah informs us in a verse that those who dare to associate other gods with Allah will be forsaken:

Do not set up any other god together with Allah and so sit there reviled and forsaken. (Surat al-Isra': 22)

THE SLEEPING BAG OF THE PARROTFISH

The fish shown in the picture is called the parrotfish since it resembles a parrot as you may have noticed. This colourful fish employs quite an unusual method to protect itself against its enemies. Especially at night, it covers its entire body with a gelatine-like substance that it itself produces. Before answering the question "why?", let's see how this substance is produced and used.

This gelatinous sheath of the parrotfish is secreted from the upper side of the gill cavity. The fish secretes the substance while it breathes. After a while this sheath covers the entire body of the fish. By doing so the fish places itself within a kind of sleeping bag and becomes protected from external

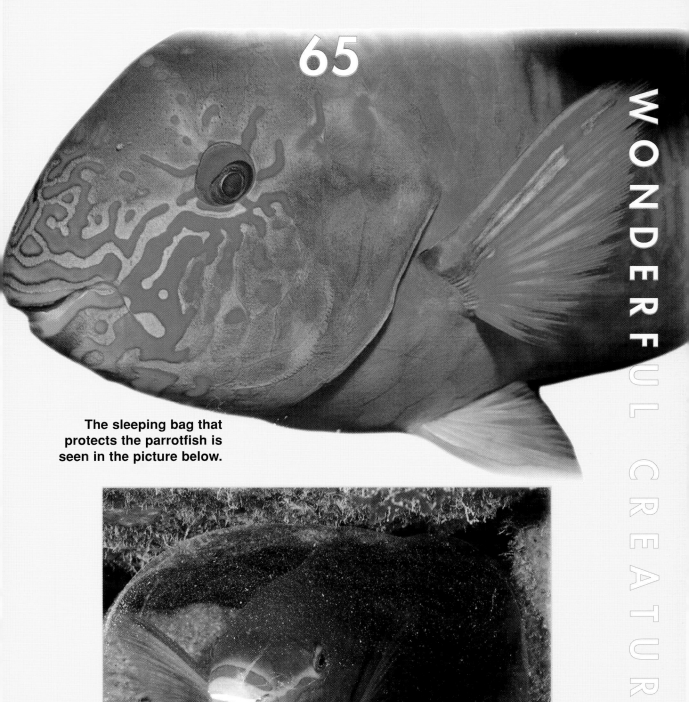

The sleeping bag that protects the parrotfish is seen in the picture below.

danger at night. This substance also enables the fish to conceal itself by camouflage. As a vital function, the transparent sleeping bag protects the fish from moray eels, one of its bitter enemies. The moray eels have an excellent sense of smell and can find their prey with it. However, the protective sheath of the parrotfish prevents the moray from perceiving its scent. The moray cannot notice the fish in the sheath even if it bumps into it while passing by.

This being the case, one should ask the following questions: How did parrotfish obtain this protective sheath that they use at night? How do they know that their leading enemy hunts by means of its sense of smell? How did they discover a substance, so essential in obstructing the moray's sense of smell so enabling them to spend the night in safety?

Obviously, one cannot expect a fish to decide to produce a chemical in its body and then to cover itself with this substance. Nor could such a thing have developed spontaneously through time. Parrotfish shown in the picture could not consciously plan to produce such a substance and could not make up such a system in their bodies of their own volition; neither could a parrotfish that lived 1,000 or 10,000 years ago.

It is a clever method of camouflage that the body of the fish is covered with gelatine, which is quite suitable for protecting the fish from its enemy. It is obvious that such a feature could come into existence only as a result of intelligent design. This intelligence is not the fish's or somebody else's, but Allah's, Who created all creatures.

THE SKILFUL CAMOUFLAGE OF SCORPION FISH

The appearance of a scorpion fish is very colourful. These fish have the same colour as the coral among which they live. As you can see in the picture, the red-and-white striped scorpion fish can conceal itself by camouflage among the coral, which are virtually the same colours. That way it escapes the attentions of predators and reduces the risk of becoming prey. Again thanks to this coloration, it can easily draw near to its own prey.

Take a careful look at the scorpion fish – seen in the picture below and the picture on the back page – and you will realise how hard it really is to notice their presence in their environments.

WONDERFUL CREATURES

WONDERFUL CREATURES

Thanks to their particular coloration, scorpion fish conceal themselves easily among the rocks.

Like scorpion fish, many other marine creatures cannot be distinguished from their environments. Their presence is only noticed when they move. These perfectly camouflaged creatures use their coloration to enable them to hunt, to reproduce and to give various signals to other creatures. But how did this harmony come about? Who made the body of a fish the same colour as the reefs in which it lives, and made it look even more like the reefs by giving it a projecting shape?

Neither chance nor the action of some other fish can possibly give a creature the same colour as the environment in which it lives. A fish, shrimp or crab can neither have the knowledge of colour nor be able to produce systems in their own bodies to change their colour. Such systems could only be designed and placed in the animal's body by a superior and powerful Being.

This almighty Being is Allah. Allah created all creatures together with the attributes they possess and in harmony with the environments in which they live. Allah has informed us in the Qur'an that He has knowledge of all creatures He created:

Does He Who created not then know? He is the All-Pervading, the All-Aware. It is He Who made the earth submissive to you, so walk its broad trails and eat what it provides. The Resurrection is to Him.
(Surat al-Mulk: 14-15)

WONDERFUL CREATURES

INTERESTING FEATURES OF SEA HORSES

You may have seen sea horses on television or in books. Their unusual horse-like appearance and their wavering pattern of swimming might have attracted your attention. Did you know that, contrary to what one might suppose, these animals are very small? Sea horses, which are 4 to 30 centimetres (1,5 to 12 inches) in size, generally live among seaweed and other plants close to the shore. The bony armour of the sea horse protects it against dangers. This armour is so tough that it is virtually impossible to crush a dried sea horse using your hands.

The sea horse's head is at a right angle to its body, which is not seen in any other fish. Consequently, sea horses swim with their bodies upright and can move their heads up and down. However, they cannot turn their heads to the side. Now let's think about the problems that other living creatures would suffer if they could not turn their heads to the right or to the left; they would be susceptible to all sorts of physical dangers. However, thanks to their special body

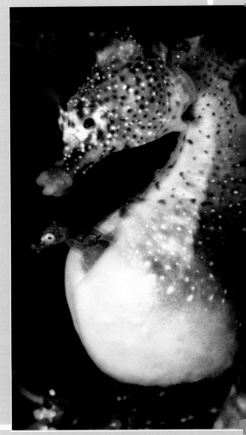

Male sea horse and its young

designs, sea horses do not experience such problems. Each eye of a sea horse can move individually and freely in all directions. That's how sea horses see around themselves easily although they cannot turn their heads to the side.

The movements of these fish in the water are also worth consideration because they swim thanks to a quite unique system. Each sea horse has a nuumber of swim bladders. Making necessary modifications in the amount of the gas filling these bladders, a sea horse can swim upwards and downwards. If these bladders are damaged and even a minor amount of gas is lost, the sea horse sinks deep down in the sea, which means death for it. One point should be noted here: the amount of gas filling the swim bladders has been arranged exactly. Therefore any change could result in the death of the animal.

What this exact arrangement reveals to us is of great importance. If sea horses can survive only with a certain amount of gas in the bladders, then they must have possessed the current features they have today when they too first emerged. In other words, sea horses have not attained their features in time as claimed by evolutionists. They were created together with all their features and characteristics out of nothing and all at once. Like all creatures in the universe, Allah created sea horses complete and perfect.

The design in sea horses, which is merely one of the numerous marine species, is an example of Allah's infinite power and endless knowledge.

DRAGONFLIES: FLIGHT MACHINES

It is possible to see dragonflies many places where water exists. If you know this insect, you might have already seen that it moves very fast and that it can make very sudden and sharp manoeuvres. But for those who are not familiar with it, let's have a look at this insect.

The appearance of a dragonfly resembles a helicopter. This insect has such a perfect talent for flight that regardless of the speed and direction it is flying in, it can suddenly stop and fly in just the opposite direction, to such an extent that it may remain suspended in the air and wait in the proper position to attack its prey. This is thanks to its wings, which it can flap very fast. When it is in this position, it can make a swift turn and head towards its prey. In fact, these are merely a few facets of its manoeuvrability that have been sources of inspiration for mankind in the construction of helicopters that are the products of today's advanced technology.

The body of a dragonfly has a ringed structure that gives the impression of its being covered with metal. A dragonfly, whose colour may vary from ice blue to claret red, has two pairs of wings on its back, one being at the front and the other at the rear. While flying, the two front wings move up as the two rear wings move down.

Sikorsky helicopters were produced in today's technology by taking this particular form of the wings of the dragonfly as model. First the picture of a dragonfly was loaded onto a computer. Considering the dragonfly's manoeuvres in the air, 2,000 special drawings were made. At the end of this study, Sikorsky came up with its new and very strong model with its advanced mobility, meant for transporting soldiers and supplies.

Have you ever noticed dragonfly's eyes? Dragonflies have perfect vision. The eyes of the dragonfly are considered the best insect eyes by scientists. A dragonfly has a pair of eyes, each one of which contains about 30,000 lenses. These eyes, which look like two hemispheres and cover half of the insect's head, provide a broad field of view. Consequently, even its back is virtually within the dragonfly's range of vision.

WONDERFUL CREATURES

These are merely a few of the features of dragonflies, described very briefly. Suppose that any one of these features of the dragonfly, say the particular type of wings, did not exist. Could this insect then make sudden manoeuvres and catch its prey? Or, if it did not have eyes that enabled it to see in every direction, could it manage to escape from its enemies?

The absence of any of the systems that a dragonfly possesses will give rise to a dysfunction of other systems. Yet, the dragonfly was created completely with all of its systems. Allah created the dragonfly perfect, like all other creatures, and it is thanks to Allah's creation that this insect lives at ease.

SECRET SHELTERS IN THE SEAS: CORALS

You may think at first sight that a coral reef is merely a heap of colourful stones. Yet, you would be mistaken because corals are living creatures. Billions of corals live together, attach themselves to others with special secretions and bring this stone-like structure into existence.

Remnants of dead corals become calcified and these residues become coral nests in time where many creatures live together. Every fish species living in a coral reef has particular characteristics. For example, fish that hunt in the daytime, such as angelfish, hide in quiet and secluded sections and cracks of the reef as the sun sets.

WONDERFUL CREATURES

Patterns of behaviour of fish that live in the coral reefs are diverse. For example, some fish, like the parrotfish we mentioned earlier, sleep deeply at nights in their sleeping bags. Some fish species, such as sticklebacks, on the other hand, are half-awake while they rest. Red mullet and some others use very bright colours in daytime and turn their skin colour pale at nights.

Sponges, corals and some fish that lay eggs also live in dead coral residues. Besides these, small crabs and shrimps climb onto coral reefs to feed on microscopic plants and animals. Fish such as sharks and moray eels that live in coral reefs use their strong sense of smell to find food in the dark.

Many different creatures that Allah created in the seas and their unique designs with miraculous features manifest our Lord's matchless artistry and infinite knowledge. In Surat an-Nahl, Allah gives some examples of the creatures He created. In the same surah He states that people should be thankful for them:

And also the things of varying colours He has created for you in the earth. There is certainly a Sign in that for people who pay heed. It is He Who made the sea subservient to you so that you can eat fresh flesh from it and bring out from it ornaments to wear. And you see the ships cleaving through it so that you can seek His bounty, and so that hopefully you will show thanks. (Surat an-Nahl: 13-14)

WONDERFUL CREATURES

LIFE IN THE DESERT

Extreme heat that reaches up to 50-60°C (122-140°F) in the daytime, freezing cold at night, drought that can last for weeks even months, and very little amount of food. You might think it impossible to live in such a place. These tough places are deserts and, contrary to what you might think, many creatures live in the desert. Below we mention some of these creatures.

One desert animal is the cream coloured fox, which is the smallest of all fox species (on the next page). The ears of this fox species are bigger than those of others. These wide ears are very useful for the fox, which lives in the sandy deserts of Africa and Arabia. For example, the fox can easily determine its prey's location thanks to its sensitive ears. Preventing excessive heating, these ears also help the animal remain cool.

Another creature that lives in the deserts is the shovel-snouted lizard (below). To cool its tail and feet, this creature

moves on hot sands as if it were dancing. Supported by its tail, it raises one of its front and one of its back legs transversely. A few seconds later, it is the turn of the other two legs. With its peculiarly shaped nose and body, the lizard moves in the mounds of sand as if swimming. Its big feet enable it to run fast on the sand without being hurt by the heat.

The desert frogs that live in Australia are like water tanks. A desert frog fills the pouches in its body with water when it rains. Then it buries itself in the sand and begins to wait for the next rain. Thanks to the water they store in their pouches, desert frogs can survive in the desert.

Have you noticed the common characteristics of desert creatures, of which we have given a few examples here? Their body structures are remarkably designed for living in the desert and they have characteristics quite distinct from other creatures. Also, these animals apparently know very well how they should act for protection from the desert heat and to cope with thirst. How could a frog or a lizard have such knowledge? How could they possess the exact body structure that they require?

Certainly animals could not know these things by themselves. They could neither create water tanks in their bodies nor generate big ears to protect themselves from the heat. In order to survive in the desert, these creatures must have had these characteristics since they came into being. Otherwise, they would soon become extinct from excessive heat, thirst or hunger. However, this does not happen. Moreover, all desert creatures on earth have the capacity to endure desert conditions. Each species has unique characteristics that enable it to survive in the desert.

All these lead us to one truth. The One Who created desert creatures together with the features they have today is Allah. Allah has power to do whatever He likes at any time He likes. In a verse of the Qur'an, Allah informs us that everything is easy for Him:

The Originator of the heavens and earth. When He decides on something, He just says to it, "Be!" and it is. (Surat al-Baqara: 117)

THE SPECIAL COOLING SYSTEM OF GAZELLES

Air conditioners protect us from cold in winter and from heat in summer. Yet, humans are not the first to discover cooling systems. Many creatures already have in their bodies cooling systems that function like air conditioners.

We may give the fast running gazelles of Africa as an example. Like many others, this animal, too, has to run away from its enemies to survive because it does not have any other defence mechanism. Yet, this fast running increases its body heat excessively, which is very dangerous for the gazelle because as the body heat increases, so does the gazelle's brain heat. However, in order for the gazelle to survive, its brain heat needs to be cooler than

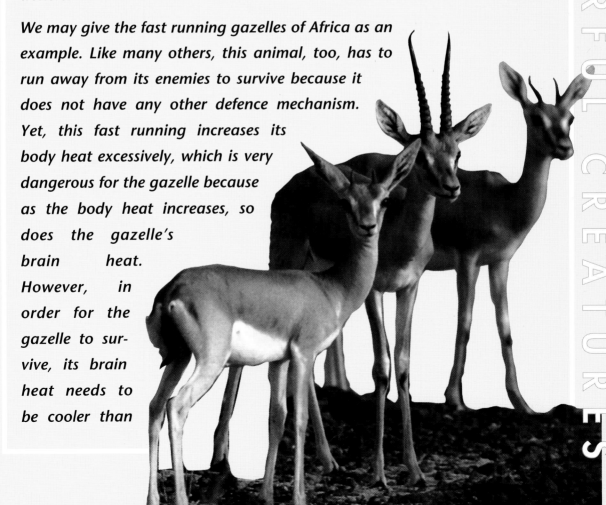

that of the body. So you may wonder how it is that gazelles don't die.

The answer to this question leads us to the fact of creation.

The brain of a gazelle is cooled by a special cooling system located on the right side of its head. Gazelles and other fast-running animals have breathing canals. Hundreds of small blood veins spread in the large blood accumulations behind these canals. The air the gazelle inhales cools this area and hence the blood that passes through these small blood veins. These small veins then unite in a single blood vessel that conveys blood to the brain. Thanks to this system, the gazelle is not affected by the sharp increase in its body heat while running.

You must have already concluded that such a perfect system could not have come into existence spontaneously over time. That is because the lack of this system, which is required for cooling the brain, would mean the death of the gazelle during its very first run.

As seen in the cooling system of gazelles, there is perfect design in living creatures. In other words, the body structure and the organs of a living thing cannot possibly come into existence over time as claimed by evolutionists.

All creatures have body structures consisting of systems that would not work even if one of the components were missing, such as the cooling system of gazelles. This proves that living creatures did not come into existence over time as a result of coincidences as evolutionists claim, but Allah created them. It is crystal clear to those who can take heed and use their intellect. Allah commands in a verse:

..."The Lord of the East and the West and everything between them if you used your intellect." (Surat ash-Shu'ara': 28)*

THE STRENGTH OF WOODPECKERS

Woodpeckers make their nests and food stores by pecking holes in trees. The speed at which a woodpecker bores into a tree with its bill is approximately 40 km/hour (25 miles/hour). This, in fact, is an extraordinary speed that could have damaged the woodpecker. However, there is a special locking system in the bird's beak so that it does not sustain injury. If this special system did not exist, the woodpecker's beak would crack in two because of the high speed. Besides, if the impact of the stroke went directly to the brain, then the bird would lose consciousness. Yet, such a thing never happens since Allah created the bird together with what it needs. The woodpecker's brain is placed at the same level as its beak. Muscles on the lower part of the beak act like "shock absorbers" and reduce the shock that occurs while boring into the tree.

What we have mentioned so far are only a few of the general characteristics of wood-peckers. Apart from those mentioned, every woodpecker species has many characteristics peculiar to itself. Now let's consider a kind of woodpecker that hides acorns in trees.

Throughout summer, the acorn woodpecker bores "holes" in a dead tree trunk because at the end of the summer it will fill these holes with acorns, on which it will feed during winter. Acting like a hammer, it drives one acorn in each hole. This takes a great deal of the wood-pecker's time because it tries to find the acorn that fits exactly into the hole it has bored. If the hole is big and the acorn is small, then the loose acorn will easily be taken by other birds. If the hole is smaller than the acorn, then the acorn will be damaged while it is being forced into the hole. Therefore, it takes some time for the woodpecker to place acorns by trial and error.

Yet there is even more that a woodpecker needs to do. As acorns dry over time they become smaller. This means that the woodpecker should replace dry acorns with fresh ones.

It should also be noted that the woodpecker does not merely store 5 to 10 acorns; an acorn woodpecker can stock approximately 50,000 acorns in a big tree.

Reflecting upon these interesting characteristics, we understand that there is a superior Power Who teaches all these things to woodpeckers. This power is Allah. Allah created the beaks of woodpeckers strong enough to drill bark. It is Allah Who taught them everything they do. There is no other god and creator besides Allah. Allah informs us that He created everything:

That is Allah, your Lord. There is no god but Him, the Creator of everything. So worship Him. He is responsible for everything.
(Surat al-An'am: 102)

A woodpecker that stores acorns in the holes in the trunk of an oak (top left) and another woodpecker species (right).

WONDERFUL CREATURES

CUTE SQUIRRELS WITH BIG CHEEKS

The squirrel you see in the picture below is the ground squirrel, also called the squirrel with cheek pouches. What distinguishes this squirrel species from others is that it carries the food that it does not consume right away in the pouches in its cheeks. The squirrel stocks this food for future use.

These cheek pouchess are actually loose folds of skin. The interior lining of these folds is bare but not humid, therefore food can be stored in these pouches for a long time without spoiling. These pouches extend to the sides.

To fill these pouches, the squirrel takes a walnut between its paws and cuts off the pointy parts on both ends with its teeth. Then it puts the walnut in one of the pouches and the next walnut in the other. Pouches are filled in this way one after the other. The animal can place four walnuts in each pouch. So, the face of the squirrel alters so that we think it is interesting and cute.

THE BIRD WITH THE LONGEST WINGS OF THE WORLD: THE ALBATROSS

Albatrosses are oceanic birds with very large wing spans, which are about 3.5 metres (11,5 feet). They spend 92% of their lives at sea and come to land only to breed. The most important characteristic of these birds is that they can fly for a very long time without stopping. They perform this difficult task by means of their style of flight.

In order to fly, it is enough for an albatross to open its wings wide open against

WONDERFUL CREATURES

On land, albatrosses walk with a waddle and appear to be very clumsy, but in the air, they are among the most graceful of sea birds.

the wind. In this way, it can fly for hours without flapping its wings at all. The bird does this by extending its wings as wide as possible, and the span of its wings reaches up to 3.5 meters (11,5 feet). This is the largest wing span among bird species.

Making use of ascending air currents and winds, the albatross moves in their direction. It proceeds in zigzags in the wind and passes from the top of one current to another. So, the albatross flies over the sea for hours without flapping its wings. But how can it perform this quite difficult task? What makes this bird so strong?

First of all, a great amount of energy is needed to keep these giant wings steadily wide open. To have a better understanding of the difficult task albatrosses carry out, let's compare albatrosses with humans. It is difficult for a man even to keep his arms open in the air for a brief time. Soon his muscles begin to ache and he lowers his arms. However, albatrosses can fly suspended in the air for hours with their wings wide open.

There is a locking system inside the wing bones of albatrosses that enables them to keep their wings open. By means of this locking system, they don't use any muscular strength. This makes flight much easier for the bird. Thanks to this special system, it can fly without stopping for days, weeks, or even for months expending only a very little amount of energy.

One merely needs to reflect for a moment to grasp that these features could not have come into existence by chance. We see the mercy and compassion of Allah upon these birds, which fly over the seas for long periods. It is Allah Who granted albatrosses all the features they need to stay alive. Allah, Who has power over all things, protects and gives albatrosses all their needs like all other creatures. Allah refers to birds in a verse:

Do they not see the birds suspended in mid-air up in the sky? Nothing holds them there except Allah. There are certainly Signs in that for people who believe. (Surat an-Nahl: 79)

WONDERFUL CREATURES

ADORNMENT ARTISTS: BOWERBIRDS

Did you know that there are birds that adorn their nests? Just like humans who decorate the place in which they live, some bird species adorn their nests too. The behaviours of these birds is certainly amazing; sometimes they embellish their nests with the decorative objects they collect or paint the walls of their nests with pink fruits.

The bowerbird, which is one of the birds that paint their nests, is a real "master of architecture". The size of a male bowerbird is like that of a pigeon. While building its nest, it arranges hundreds of thin branches in two lines each facing one another, as seen in the picture. This way it builds a bower. It piles up all the stuff it picks from the environment in front of this bower. This may even be a butterfly's wing, a bird's feather, a car key or some wrapping paper. This bird is particularly interested in blue objects. As you can see in the picture, it has gathered all the blue objects it could find in its nest.

In addition to this, it uses some other means of decoration as well. The bowerbird also paints the walls of its nest. What is more, it prepares the paint itself. Do you want to know how? It gathers plants in different colours and paints the walls by using their extracts. Sometimes it uses coal, which it mixes with its saliva. It also paints the nest's walls, which are made up of branches, with a piece of bark it chews in its mouth.

Allah is the Creator of all bird species, including those we don't ever see like bowerbirds and those that we frequently see like pigeons and gulls. Allah the All-Glorious teaches a little bird how to build and decorate its nest. What we should do is to reflect thoroughly on such characteristics of animals to have a better understanding of Allah's boundless power. Allah states in a verse:

And He has made everything in the heavens and everything on the earth subservient to you. It is all from Him. There are certainly Signs in that for people who reflect. (Surat al-Jathiyya: 13)

BIRDS WHICH LAY FOUNDATIONS FOR THEIR YOUNG

Megapodes live in Australia and build very special nests for their eggs. The male megapode digs a large hole and fills it with wet, decaying plant matter. The bird has a very important and specific reason to do so. Bacteria in the decaying plant matter produce heat and thus warm the nest. In order to keep the temperature steady, the male makes ventilation openings and continuously checks the temperature of the nest by sticking its beak through these openings. It also makes a funnel shaped opening on the surface of the heap of vegetation. This opening lets rainwater leak into the heap during winter and thus keeps it moist.

Once the nest is ready, the female comes along and lays its eggs in the hole. However, the temperature of the nest increases continuously during the summer, upon which the male megapode covers the nest with sand. This way, it tries to prevent transmission of heat to the nest.

Now, let us ask a question. Before you read these paragraphs, did you know that heat is released by decaying plants? It is natural for you not to know about this unless you have already read a relevant book. Many people do not know. Yet, megapodes have this knowledge. What is more, they make use of this knowledge for the benefit of their young.

Well then, but how could a bird do such delicate calculations and sensitive measurements? How could it take technical precautions according to the results it achieves? Why does it bear such a troublesome task for its young?

In order to do all these, a bird needs to have technical knowledge like that of an engineer and the intellectual function of a healthy human being.

Certainly, a bird does not have the reason and the brain to act like an intelligent and learned person. There is a Power Who directs and makes the megapode carry out these tasks, which require intellect. This power is Allah, Who created everything in the most beautiful way.

As you read this book, you immediately see that these creatures cannot do all these wonderful things by themselves and you understand that Allah created all of them. Yet, there are some people who refuse to accept this fact, which you have understood at once. Allah has informs us of these people in the Qur'an. In Surat ar-Rad, Allah states:

Say: "Who is the Lord of the heavens and the earth?'" Say: "Allah." Say: "So why have you taken protectors apart from Him who possess no power to help or harm themselves?" Say: "Are the blind and seeing equal? Or are darkness and light the same? Or have they assigned partners to Allah Who create as He creates, so that all creating seems the same to them?" Say: "Allah is the Creator of everything. He is the One, the All-Conquering." (Surat ar-Ra'd: 16)

THE POWERFUL MEMORY OF JAYS

Jays gather acorns and bury them in the ground for future use. Sometimes they bury up to a thousand acorns in a day. Everything in a forest looks alike. This is why it is difficult even for man to find a certain place in a forest. So how can jays find the places where they have hidden their acorns? They act intelligently and mark these places using tree branches or pieces of stone. Still, it is quite difficult to find something buried in a forest. However experiments have revealed that these birds can find their acorns even nine months later. It is a miracle of creation that these birds have such a powerful memory that they can mark the places where they hide their food and then remember these places.

It is certainly not possible to explain the decision of a jay, which does not have intellect as we understand it, to hide acorns by burying them in the ground or marking these secret places to find them in the future as occurring by coincidence.

Burying a thousand acorns and marking their places with stones and branches in an orderly way is certainly something that a bird cannot achieve on its own. It is very natural for a bird to eat an acorn as soon as it finds it. However, only an intelligent being can save it for future use, mark the place where it is hidden and know this mark later.

A bird cannot do any of these by itself. Therefore, we understand that there is a Being Who possesses endless wisdom, has power over all things and makes jays do all the things they do. This superior wisdom belongs to Allah, Who created everything perfectly in an order and rules them all. This bird hides its food only because Allah wills so, and can find it only if Allah wills. As in every creation of Allah, we witness the signs of His perfect creation in this bird too.

THE ARMOURED TANKS OF THE ANIMAL KINGDOM

These animals of South America, which are called armadillos, have a very interesting appearance because of the armour covering their bodies. These creatures feed on insects and usually search for food by digging in the ground. Armadillos have a keen sense of smell. Perceiving the scent of food, the armadillo embeds its nose in the ground and delves into it in haste as if it is afraid of losing the

scent. One might be surprised to see how the armadillo manages to breathe while doing this. However, armadillos do not breathe at that moment. Indeed, they are capable of holding their breath for up to six minutes. This prevents them from choking while digging into the ground.

Thanks to this ability to hold their breath for a long time, which Allah bestowed on them, armadillos can dig into the ground and find their food. This example manifests Allah's mercy and compassion towards the living creatures that He created. In a verse, Allah introduces Himself to us:

Truly your Lord is the Almighty, the Most Merciful. (Surat ash-Shu'ara': 9)

MIGRATORY BIRDS THAT CAN FLY EVEN IN THE DARK OF THE NIGHT

Many bird species travel thousands of kilometres every year to regions where they can find rich sources of food and where they can lay their eggs and raise their offspring. Allah refers to the flight of birds in a verse:

Have they not looked at the birds above them, with wings outspread and folded back? Nothing holds them up but the All-Merciful. He sees all things. (Surat al-Mulk: 19)

WONDERFUL CREATURES

Many aquatic birds successfully make long distance flights. This is thanks to their strong body structure and to the communication between them. Aquatic birds communicate with each other while flying by means of singing and producing different sounds. This holds every member of the flock together even in the dark of the night no matter how large they are in number.

Every member of the flock knows where the others are. Scientists suppose that water birds use the sun to reckon their location. Once they are close to their destination, they recognise certain marks. This is similar to your using

Birds in flight are among the signs that Allah mentions in the Qur'an and urges us to reflect upon.

certain streets and buildings to find your way home. Likewise, aquatic birds follow rivers, mountains and other landmarks. Some aquatic birds can fly without stopping night and day during their migration.

The skill in finding direction is peculiar to human beings who have intellect. Man can find direction by using some technical instruments or by the help of the sky. But, how do birds find their direction? How can they make use of the sun's position or of some other signs?

It is Allah the Almighty Who bestowed this wonderful skill upon birds, and created a special communication system among them. Allah manifests His artistry in creation with all the characteristics and features He creates in living things. In the verse "Have they not looked at the birds above them, with wings outspread and folded back?" Allah draws our attention to birds' flight. He wants us to reflect on these abilities He has bestowed upon birds. Thinking this way, we come across intelligent behaviour and perfect bodily systems that creatures cannot possibly develop on their own. Reflecting on what we see, we understand that Allah teaches them what to do.

Then certainly reflect upon such facts and share your thoughts with other people. Make sure they grasp Allah's exaltedness and that it is Allah Who created everything.

WONDERFUL CREATURES

CLEANING WORKERS OF THE SEAS

What occurs to you if you see a small fish that is about to enter the mouth of a big fish? You think that the big fish will swallow the small fish, and you wonder why the small fish comes so close to it.

It is undoubtedly unusual that the big fish lets the small fish swim around it, does not attack it and does not care about its swimming in its mouth or through its gills. It is, however, possible to see such scenes in the oceans a lot. It is not only some small fish that fearlessly swim around the big fish. Sometimes shrimps, too, may be seen near the mouths of big fish. These are cleaner shrimps whose job is to clean some of the big fish.

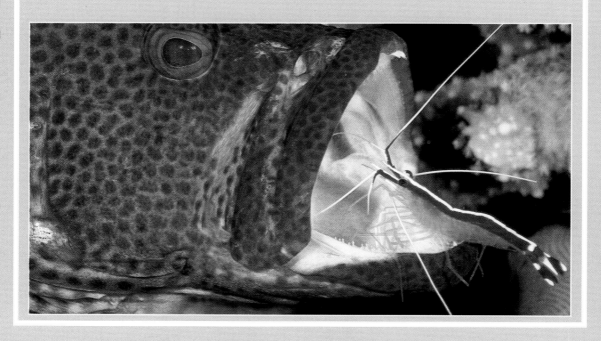

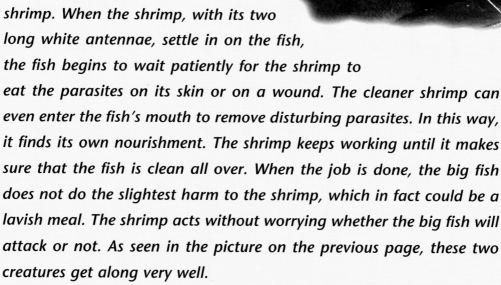

There are many kinds of cleaner shrimps. The one seen in the picture is one of them. The red and white stripes of the shrimp make it visible like a lighthouse and help the fish which is in need of cleaning find the shrimp. When the shrimp, with its two long white antennae, settle in on the fish, the fish begins to wait patiently for the shrimp to eat the parasites on its skin or on a wound. The cleaner shrimp can even enter the fish's mouth to remove disturbing parasites. In this way, it finds its own nourishment. The shrimp keeps working until it makes sure that the fish is clean all over. When the job is done, the big fish does not do the slightest harm to the shrimp, which in fact could be a lavish meal. The shrimp acts without worrying whether the big fish will attack or not. As seen in the picture on the previous page, these two creatures get along very well.

Concepts like "getting along well", "giving guarantee" are peculiar to humans who have intellect and intelligence, and therefore cannot be valid for these creatures. Yet, Allah, Who has control and power over all things, taught these creatures to behave so, to trust and co-operate with each other. So, they lead their lives easily.

WONDERFUL CREATURES

THE NOISY CICADA

The cicada is a noisy insect. It produces ticks, buzzes and whines by means of a system in its body. There are a pair of membranous organs at the base of the insect's abdomen. The cicada produces that well-known sound by vibrating these drumlike membranes. When these membranes are pulled and released by the muscles to which they are attached, a sound similar to that of an empty tin is produced. The insect repeats this pull-and-release process 500 times a second. Considering that you can only close and reopen your eyes once in a second, you can readily see how difficult it is to perform this task 500 times a second.

With the opening and closing of the extended part that exists on the lower part of the insect's thorax, the sound level may be increased and decreased. The human ear cannot perceive these openings and closings, which occur in a tenth of a second, so we do not notice that the sound is interrupted and we think that the buzzing song of the cicada is continuous.

CLEANER BIRDS

The birds you see in the pictures are cleaner birds, which are called oxpeckers. These birds feed on the parasites that live on the hides of animals such as rhinoceroses, elephants and zebras. For this reason, these birds' perching upon them, even upon their heads does not bother such animals.

This partnership benefits both sides a lot. This way, the animals get rid of the bothersome parasites and are also warned by the birds, which screech in case of danger. In return, the birds obtain food and even hair to cover the inside of their nests.

Allah created this mutually beneficial relationship between animals. Allah created all these creatures along with the creatures that meet their needs.

WONDERFUL CREATURES

POND SKATERS THAT WALK ON WATER

It is impossible for human beings to walk on the surface of the water. Yet, some creatures can do so by means of the special body structures that Allah has given to them. For example, an insect species called the pond skater walks on water by pressing its thin, long legs into a kind of elastic skin on the surface of the water. As the legs of the insect push the water, a small hole is formed on the surface. This way the insect spreads its body weight over quite a wide area.

Observation and examination reveal that the legs of the pond skater do not break the surface of the water. In other words, its feet do not enter the water. Therefore, the pond skater is able to walk on the surface while other creatures cannot.

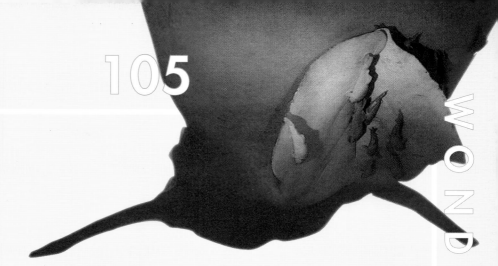

The appearance
of the suckerfish
from below.

TENACIOUS SUCKERFISH

What is special about suckerfish is that they use vessels to get around the ocean. For this, they may use sharks or ships. The dorsal fin of the fish is like an oval sucking disc. It can move along with anything it attaches itself to, whether animate or inanimate. Whatever the creature to which it is attached does or no matter how fast it swims, the suckerfish does not become detached from it. In the picture above, suckerfish that are attached to the underside of a shark are seen. Allah knows where every creature is and what it does. In a verse, Allah states:

What is in the heavens and in the earth belongs to Allah. Allah encompasses all things. (Surat an-Nisa: 126)

WONDERFUL CREATURES

WONDERFUL CREATURES

WALKING FISH WITH RED LIPS

The batfish with red lips is the only fish in the world that walks on its four fins. Fins that are designed so as to enable walking, a weird looking nose and big red lips make the appearance of this fish quite unusual. What enables the batfish to walk on the sea floor like a human being is its pectoral and pelvic fins. Using these fins, the batfish can easily stand on the sea floor and walk on the tips of its fins.

Apart from this ability, the batfish with red lips has another interesting feature. It has small appendages below its nose, which it uses as a fishing line to deceive other fish. Batfish are carnivorous. Using their fishing lines, they prey upon other fish, crabs, larvae and cockles.

The complex design in these little fish that live at the bottom of the sea shows us one of the examples of Allah's artistry.

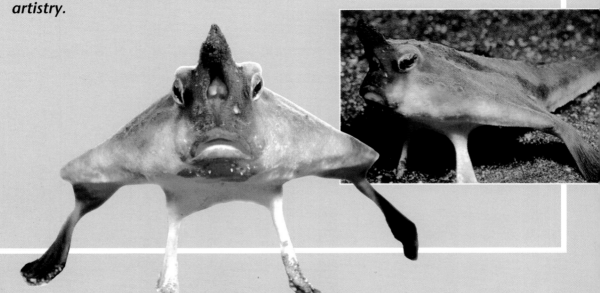

COLOURFUL HERONS

Herons can be seen at almost any place where water exists. The big blue heron seen in the picture is the tallest wild bird that lives in North America. Blue herons, whose colour attracts attention, live alone other than when they make their nests.

The nesting places where herons congregate are usually in remote hidden areas that are hard for humans to reach. Hank herons, another heron species, have various colours during spring. New colours appear around the colourful beaks of the adults only during the time of nesting.

Allah created birds in very different colours. We enjoy looking at the eye-catching colours in a bird's feathers. This wide variety of colours in birds is one of the evidences of Allah's mar-

vellous creation. In the Qur'an, Allah relates that it is He Who creates the colours:

Do you not see that Allah sends down water from the sky and by it We bring forth fruits of varying colours? And in the mountains there are streaks of white and red, of varying shades, and rocks of deep jet black. And mankind and beasts and livestock are likewise of varying colours. Only those of His slaves with knowledge have fear of Allah. Allah is Almighty, Ever-Forgiving. (Surah Fatir: 27-28)

PARAKEETS THAT CAN SURVIVE A MONTH WITHOUT WATER

Wild parakeets live in the plains of Australia where it rarely rains. Since they meet their need for water from the seeds on which they feed, these birds can easily survive without drinking water for a month in very dry seasons. Water is vital to wild parakeets. For this reason, they can organise all their lives according to climatic conditions. For example, if water is insufficient, they stop breeding and begin to search for new places with water. As soon as they find a sufficiently big body of water, they begin to lay their eggs.

It is only by the inspiration of Allah that parakeets organise their lives in compliance with climatic conditions. Since the continuance of their species is essential, they do not take any risks and stop breeding at once. Our Lord, Who knows everything and is well aware of His creatures, inspires them to behave that wisely. In a verse, Allah says:

The seven heavens and the earth and everyone in them glorify Him. There is nothing which does not glorify Him with praise but you do not understand their glorification. He is All-Forbearing, Ever-Forgiving.
(Surat al-Isra': 44)

WONDERFUL CREATURES

THE STRUCTURE OF BIRDS' FEATHERS

The most important difference that distinguishes birds from other creatures is surely their ability to fly. Birds can fly thanks to their feathers, which in fact have a very special structure.

A bird's feather is a light structure that has lift force and can easily regain its original shape. If we examine a bird's feather under a microscope, we see a marvellous design. In the middle part of the feather is a hard central shaft having a vane of paired branches called barbs on either side. These barbs, whose lengths and softness vary, enable the bird to fly in the air.

As we examine in further detail, we encounter even more interesting structures. From each barb minute hairs called "barbules" project. Barbules cannot be seen with the naked eye. On these barbules are little hooks. The barbules are interlocked by these hooks like a zipper.

The hooks are clamped together like the two rows of a zipper. The barbules held together by hooks are so close to each other that even smoke cannot escape through them. If these hooks are somehow unlocked, it is enough for the bird to shake itself or to put its feathers in order with its beak, to make the feathers return to their previous state.

In order to survive, birds should always keep their feathers clean, neat and ready for use. For the care of their feathers, they use the oil sacs that are at the bottom of their tails. They take some oil with their beak, and then clean and polish their feathers. In swimming birds, this oil prevents water from reaching their skin when they are in the water or in the rain.

In addition, birds can prevent loss of body heat by ruffling their feathers in cold weather. In hot weather, on the other hand, they keep their body cool by smoothing their feathers.

WONDERFUL CREATURES

Look at a bird's feather under a microscope, and you will see the interlocked and hooked structure of the feather.

Each group of feathers in a particular part of the body has particular functions. For example the down feathers and the feathers that lie along the wings and tail have different structures. Large tail feathers are used for steering as well as for braking. As the wing feathers are spread wide while flying, the surface area is expanded and lift force increased. When the bird flaps its wing downwards, these feathers come closer and prevent air passing through. As the wings move up, the feathers open wide and permit air to pass through them. In order to maintain their ability to fly, birds moult their feathers at certain times of the year. Large torn or worn out feathers that do not function properly any more are renewed quickly.

This detailed structure exists in the feathers of every bird. All of them have the features that enable birds to fly. One who reflects on what is explained here and uses his intellect will notice the design in birds and will understand that this design is Allah's creation. Even thinking about this attribute of birds alone is enough to understand how mighty Allah is.

It is related in the Qur'an that believers reflect on the creation of Allah:

The kingdom of the heavens and earth belongs to Allah. Allah has power over all things. In the creation of the heavens and the earth, and the alternation of night and day, there are Signs for people with intelligence: those who remember Allah, standing, sitting and lying on their sides, and reflect on the creation of the heavens and the earth (and say): 'Our Lord, You have not created this for nothing. Glory be to You! So safeguard us from the punishment of the Fire. (Surah Al 'Imran: 189-191)

BIRDS' TECHNIQUES OF SOARING

It requires a great deal of energy to fly. However, birds are small creatures and the energy they can store in their bodies is limited. Birds obtain most of the energy they need by means of applying special flying techniques. Gliding in the air without flapping their wings is one of the techniques that they use most. For example, vultures employ a special method based on rising heat waves in order to glide at a convenient altitude. Gliding from one heat wave to another, they can fly over a vast area in a day.

Migratory birds, too, make use of gliding techniques to save energy. Storks, for example, use heat waves to fly during migration. White storks of central Europe migrate to spend winter in Africa and cover a distance of about 7,000 kilometres (4,350 miles). If they were to flap their wings

all the way to their destination, they would have to take four breaks during the journey. Yet, white storks complete their journey in three weeks by gliding between the heat waves for 6-7 hours a day and thus saving most of their energy.

Since the sea warms up more slowly than the land, there are no heat waves over the sea. For this reason, migratory birds prefer to migrate over land instead of making long sea journeys. You might have seen flocks of storks that cover the sky at certain times of the year. This is because storks, too, prefer to migrate over land. You may not be aware of the fact that there isn't any warm air over the sea but storks know it very well.

On the other hand, albatrosses, seagulls and other sea birds save energy by using air currents caused by high waves. These sea birds that fly over the waves benefit from the lift force of the air that turns upwards.

As seen in the examples given here, all birds are cognisant of which techniques they will use, where they will go and which route they will take. No confusion arises for those that fly by using warm air currents and those that fly by using air currents caused by the waves. This is because Allah inspires every creature with the knowledge it needs. In the Qur'an, Allah points out birds' movements in the air and states:

Do you not see that everyone in the heavens and earth glorifies Allah, as do the birds with their outspread wings? Each one knows its prayer and glorification. Allah knows what they do. (Surat an-Nur: 41)

THE WATER BIRD THAT CUTS THROUGH THE WATER LIKE SCISSORS

Most birds cannot fly if their wings come into contact with water because water causes their feathers to stick to each other, which disables the bird moving its wings. However, although aquatic birds dive into water all day, nothing happens to them. You must be wondering how and why, are you not?

There is a special oil on the wings of water birds that prevents feathers from sticking to each other when wet. This is how these birds can dive into water without trouble. However, the skimmer, a water bird species, lacks this oil. Therefore, unlike other water birds, it cannot dive into water to hunt. How, then, will it find its nourishment when it cannot enter water?

Allah, the All-Merciful, All-Compassionate, has created the lower beak of the bird longer than its upper beak. The tip of the longer, lower beak is sensitive to touch. In addition, the wings of this aquatic bird have been designed so perfectly that it can glide just above the sea for a long time without flapping its wings at all. While flying, it breaks the surface of the water using its lower beak like scissors. As soon as the sensitive tip of the beak touches its prey, the bird immediately notices and catches it. This bird is one of the evidences that Allah is the Originator of all creatures.

... He knows everything in the land and sea. No leaf falls without His knowing it. There is no seed in the darkness of the earth, and nothing moist or dry which is not in a Clear Book. (Surat al-An'am: 59)

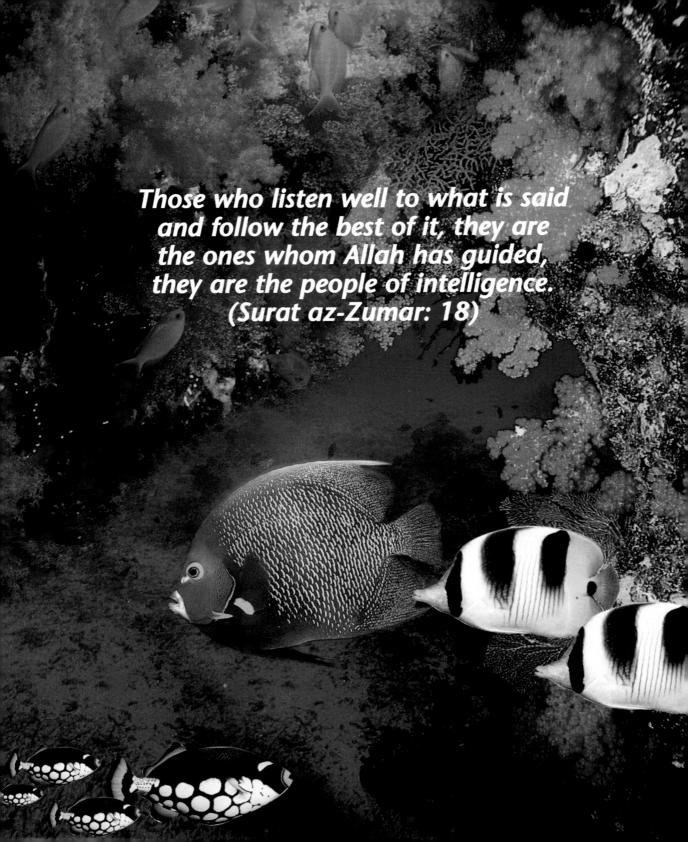

Those who listen well to what is said and follow the best of it, they are the ones whom Allah has guided, they are the people of intelligence.
(Surat az-Zumar: 18)

CUTTLEFISH LIKE JET ENGINES

Although named a "fish", unlike other fish, the cuttlefish do not have bones in their bodies. You may have wondered how these boneless fish move along in water. Indeed, cuttlefish use quite an unusual means of locomotion. The body of a cuttlefish, which is composed of soft tissues, is covered with a thick layer of skin. By means of muscles below this layer, a cuttlefish collects water within its body and moves by squirting this water out.

The system of the cuttlefish based on squirting water is quite complicated. There is a pocket-like opening on each side of the creature's head. The water is drawn through these openings into a cylinder-like cavity. Then the cuttlefish jets out this water from a narrow pipe immediately under its head with great pressure. This enables the animal to move swiftly in the opposite direction and flee from predators because it can accelerate suddenly. You may be wondering what would happen if the speed was not high enough. In this case the cuttlefish sprays a dark coloured liquid produced in the ani-

mal's body towards its enemy. This spray of ink confuses the predator for a few seconds, which is enough for the cuttlefish to flee. It flees from the place and disappears in the spray of ink.

As all other living creatures, this feature of the cuttlefish is the creation of Allah, the Creator of everything. Allah informs us that there is no other god besides Him :

Exalted be Allah, the King, the Real. There is no god but Him, Lord of the Noble Throne. (Surat az-Zumar: 10)

GREYLAG GEESE

Greylag geese can fly at high altitudes of about 8,000 metres (5 miles). This is in fact quite a difficult task since many creatures cannot breathe at such altitudes because of the deficiency in the amount of oxygen available at high altitudes. This deficiency makes respiration difficult. That is the reason why we can hardly breathe when we climb up a high mountain. Flying at an altitude that has a rarefied atmosphere, the bird needs to flap its wings faster. In order to move its wings more, the bird will expend more

Everything in the heavens and the earth belongs to Allah. He knows what you are engaged upon. On the Day when they are returned to Him, He will inform them of what they did. Allah has knowledge of all things.
(Surat an-Nur: 64)

oxygen, which makes the situation even more difficult for it. However, these birds do not experience any difficulty even while they are flying at altitudes of thousands of meters. That is thanks to the special creation of their lungs, which make the most of the rare oxygen at high altitudes.

Functioning in a different way than those of other creatures, these birds' lungs enable them to obtain more energy from the rarefied atmosphere. And this is one of the signs of Allah's perfect creation.

A MATCHLESS SECURITY SYSTEM

Some creatures living near the surface of water are susceptible to dangers both from above the water and from beneath them. These creatures have an incredible means of security; they are transparent. As you can see in the pictures, they are unnoticed by their enemies. Likewise, crab, shrimp and fish larvae are created almost completely transparent.

Obviously these creatures could not possibly have considered the environment they lived in and then adopted an appropriate colour. Besides, how would these animals know that they need to be protected? How could they be aware of the presence of predators and conclude that they would not be noticed if they were transparent?

Allah, Who creates everything perfectly, created these little defenceless creatures with a perfect design. Allah watches over and protects all things. Our

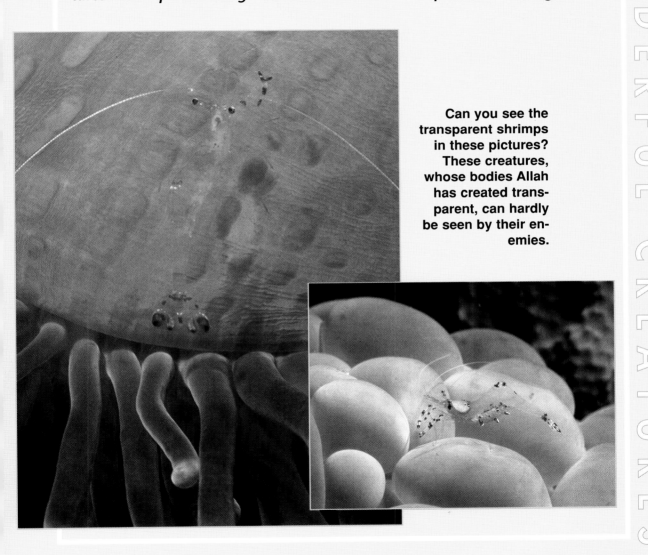

Can you see the transparent shrimps in these pictures? These creatures, whose bodies Allah has created transparent, can hardly be seen by their enemies.

WONDERFUL CREATURES

compassionate Lord created a particular way of protection for each being. And these creatures are protected from predators thanks to their transparency. Allah creates all creatures completely and perfectly. It is related in verses that Allah's creation is matchless:

He Who created the seven heavens in layers. You will not find any flaw in the creation of the All-Merciful. Look again – do you see any gaps? Then look again and again. Your sight will return to you dazzled and exhausted! (Surat al-Mulk: 3-4)

CONCLUSION

Children,

In this book, we looked at some examples of the miraculous creatures that Allah created. Exposing the amazing features and some intelligent behaviour patterns in these creatures, we aimed to help you comprehend once again that these could not have come into existence by themselves and that Allah created them all.

As you are well aware, the examples given in this book are only a small sample of the creatures living in the world. There are many other

WONDERFUL CREATURES

species, which are millions in number, living in the sea, on land or in the air. All these creatures have different bodily systems and different patterns of behaviour. For example a bird never acts like a tiger, and the way an elephant feeds is not the same as that of a duck. A crocodile lives both in water and on land, whereas a monkey cannot live in water. In short, the characteristics and features of species are particular to themselves; their appearance, the way they feed and care for their offspring is different from each other.

You already know that it is our Lord Who created all these creatures together with their particular characteristics and Who taught them all the things they do. If you've not known before now, then you have definitely understood this fact as you read this book. Now tell what you've learnt to

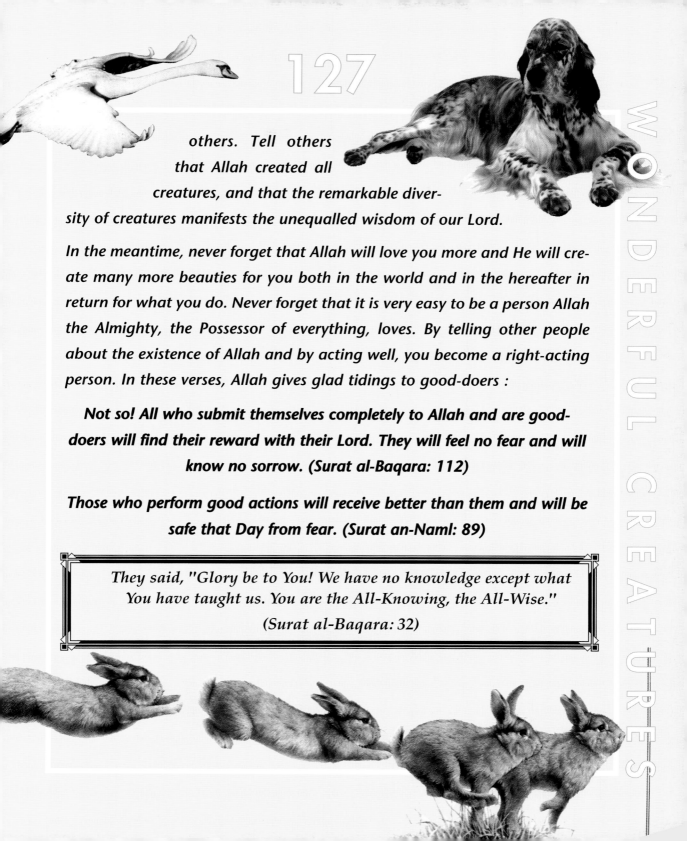

others. Tell others that Allah created all creatures, and that the remarkable diversity of creatures manifests the unequalled wisdom of our Lord.

In the meantime, never forget that Allah will love you more and He will create many more beauties for you both in the world and in the hereafter in return for what you do. Never forget that it is very easy to be a person Allah the Almighty, the Possessor of everything, loves. By telling other people about the existence of Allah and by acting well, you become a right-acting person. In these verses, Allah gives glad tidings to good-doers :

Not so! All who submit themselves completely to Allah and are good-doers will find their reward with their Lord. They will feel no fear and will know no sorrow. (Surat al-Baqara: 112)

Those who perform good actions will receive better than them and will be safe that Day from fear. (Surat an-Naml: 89)

They said, "Glory be to You! We have no knowledge except what You have taught us. You are the All-Knowing, the All-Wise."
(Surat al-Baqara: 32)

Also by Harun Yahya

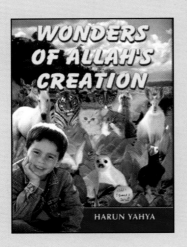

Wonders of Allah's Creation

Have you ever asked yourself questions like these: How did our earth come into existence? Where were you before you were born? How did oceans, trees, animals appear on earth? Who was the first human being? In this book you will find the true answers to these questions.

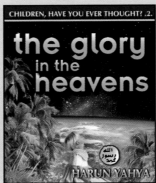

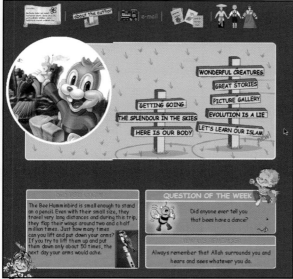

www.truthsforkids.com
www.for-children.com

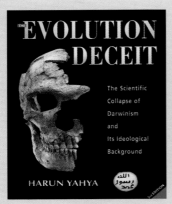

Many people think that Darwin's Theory of Evolution is a proven fact. Contrary to this conventional wisdom, recent developments in science completely disprove the theory. The only reason Darwinism is still foisted on people by means of a worldwide propaganda campaign lies in the ideological aspects of the theory. All secular ideologies and philosophies try to provide a basis for themselves by relying on the theory of evolution.

This book clarifies the scientific collapse of the theory of evolution in a way that is detailed but easy to understand. It reveals the frauds and distortions committed by evolutionists to "prove" evolution. Finally it analyzes the powers and motives that strive to keep this theory alive and make people believe in it.

Anyone who wants to learn about the origin of living things, including mankind, needs to read this book.

238 PAGES WITH 166 PICTURES IN COLOUR

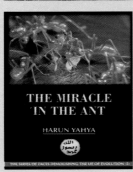

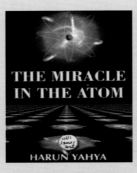
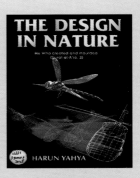

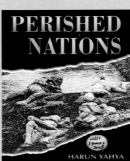
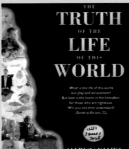

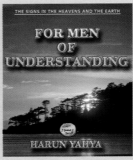
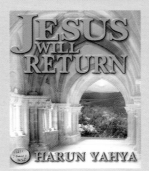

VIDEO FILMS AND AUDIO CASSETTES
BASED ON THE WORKS OF HARUN YAHYA

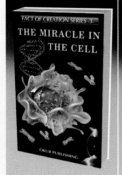

The works of Harun Yahya are also produced in the form of documentary films and cassettes, which are available as VHS, VCD or DVD. This page includes some of these documentaries.

Audio presentations based on the works of Harun Yahya are produced in the form of tape-cassettes. The titles in this series include The Theory of Evolution The Fact of Creation, The Creation of the Universe/The Balances in the Earth, The Miracle in the Cell/The Miracle of Birth, The Miracle in the Eye/The Miracle in the Ear, The Design in Animals/The Design in Plants, The Miracle in the Honeybee/The Miracle in the Ant, The Miracle in the Mosquito/The Miracle in the Spider, Self-Sacrifice in Living Things/Migration and Orientation, The Miracle of Creation in DNA, Miracles of the Qur'an.

HARUN YAHYA ON THE INTERNET

www.harunyahya.com
e-mail: info@harunyahya.com

OTHER SITES:

www.evolutiondocumentary.com
www.darwinismrefuted.com
www.jesuswillreturn.com
www.endoftimes.net
www.unionoffaiths.com
www.creationofuniverse.com
www.evolutiondeceit.com
secretbeyondmatter.com

www.miraclesofthequran.com
www.islamdenouncesterrorism.com
www.islamdenouncesantisemitism.com
www.perishednations.com
www.for-children.com
www.insight-magazine.com
www.freebookcenter.com
www.bookglobal.net